CW01379232

HOW TO BE A BOSS WITCH

First published in 2026 by Welbeck Illustrated
An imprint of Headline Publishing Group Limited

Copyright © 2026 Headline Publishing Group Limited

Illustrations © Fee Greening Limited
Icons on pp. 24-5, 29, 47, 91, 102, 130-1, 143 © Shutterstock.com

Text by Vicki Vrint
With thanks to Isla McKay

1

Apart from any use permitted under UK copyright law, this publication may only be reproduced, stored, or transmitted, in any form, or by any means, with prior permission in writing of the publishers or, in the case of reprographic production, in accordance with the terms of licences issued by the Copyright Licensing Agency.
Cataloguing in Publication Data is available from the British Library

ISBN 978-1-0354-2998-1

Printed and bound in Dubai

MIX
Paper | Supporting responsible forestry
FSC® C104740

Headline's policy is to use papers that are natural, renewable and recyclable products and made from wood grown in well-managed forests and other controlled sources. The logging and manufacturing processes are expected to conform to the environmental regulations of the country of origin.

HEADLINE PUBLISHING GROUP LIMITED
An Hachette UK Company
Carmelite House
50 Victoria Embankment
London EC4Y 0DZ

www.headline.co.uk
www.hachette.co.uk

The authorized representative in the EEA is Hachette Ireland,
8 Castlecourt Centre, Dublin 15, D15 XTP3, Ireland (email: info@hbgi.ie)

HOW TO BE A BOSS WITCH

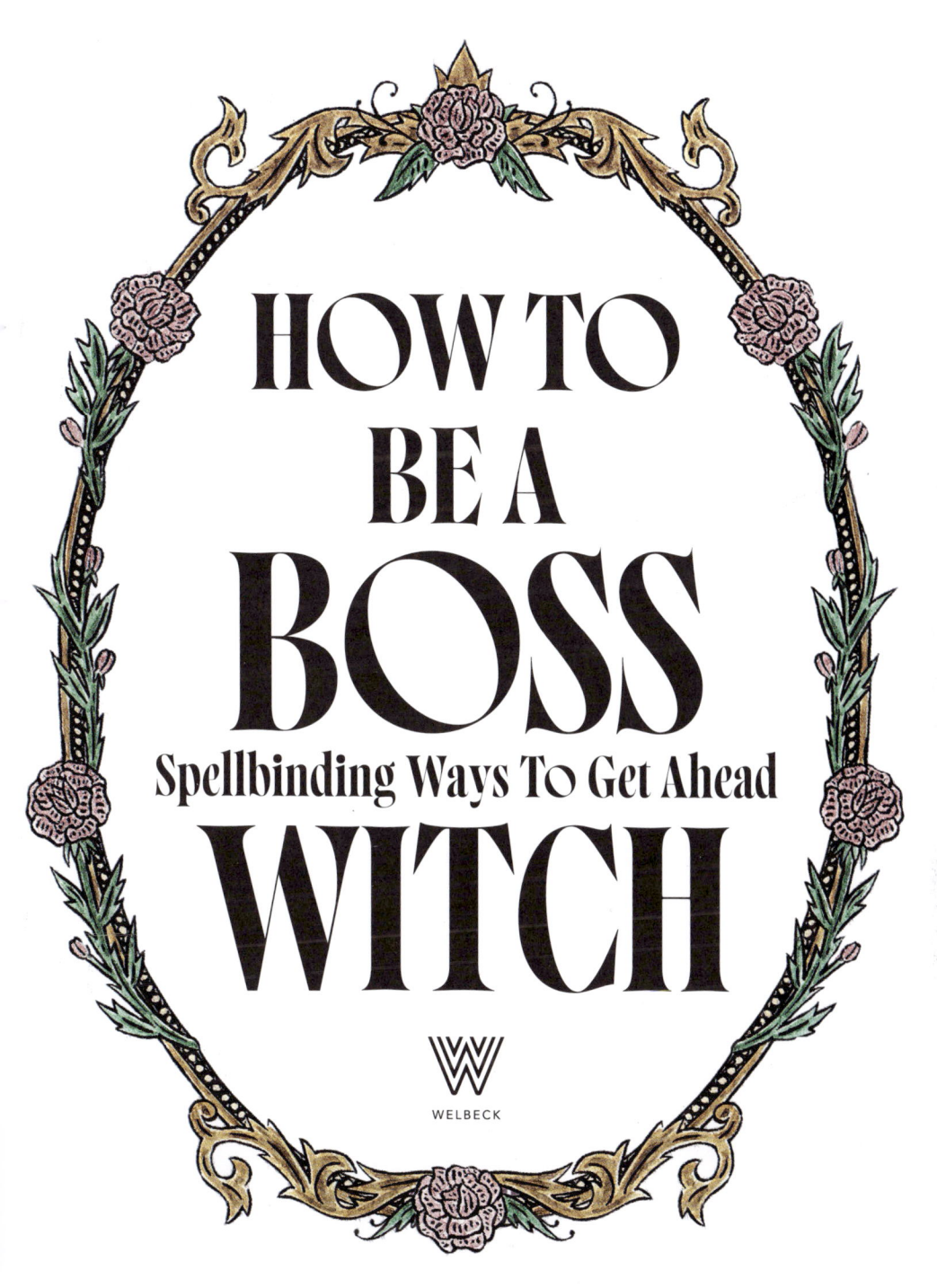

Spellbinding Ways To Get Ahead

WELBECK

WITH ILLUSTRATIONS BY FEE GREENING

CONTENTS

INTRODUCTION   6

1   WITCH WAY?   8
Spotting signs and finding direction through oracle cards, symbolism and scrying

2   DIVINE TIMING   22
The best times to cast spells

3   WITCHES GET PROMOTED   36
Ways to be seen and heard

4   VERY IMPORTANT WITCH   50
Getting ahead, influencing people and knowing your true worth

5   WITCHES WHO LUNCH   66
Lunchbreak spells

6	**THERE'S NO (EVIL) 'I' IN TEAM** *Banish bad vibes and nurture a positive atmosphere*	80
7	**SHOW ME THE MONEY** *Money and prosperity spells*	94
8	**WHEREVER I LAY MY BROOM ...** *Witching under the radar*	108
	SAFE HEXING	120
9	**GHOSTS IN THE BOARDROOM** *Exorcise energy vampires and ghosts of bad experiences*	122
10	**PAYBACK'S A WITCH** *Time to really stand up for yourself*	138
	WITCHING WARNINGS	154
	BOSS WITCH BLESSINGS	156
	INDEX	157

INTRODUCTION

Dear Reader

Welcome to the world of the Boss Witch – a book filled with spells, recipes and rituals to help you achieve your career goals and make your workplace a great place to be. Whether you want to go for a promotion, conjure up a pay rise or deal with a tricky colleague, there's a spell here to assist you, along with any scenarios you may encounter in the workplace and witchy ways to handle them.

Witchcraft is the perfect tool to help you progress at work. You're already full of magic (of course!), but spells can channel your intentions, give them a boost and get results.

Witchcraft is also empowering. It can be a way of taking back control, making your truth heard, or even containing a toxic person or situation. There are hexing spells throughout the book for binding, banishing or freezing out someone who is causing you distress.

Making magic

If you're new to witchcraft, there are a few things you should do at the start of every spell or ritual. (I'll describe them here rather than repeat them on every page.)

First, cleanse your materials and the area where you'll be working, both physically and metaphysically, to get rid of any negative energy. You can do this by smudging with sage or burning incense. Alternatively, you could use sound by ringing a bell.

Cast a circle before you begin spell casting. Visualize a protective barrier forming around you as you call in the grounding power of the Earth element at the north. Turn to the east and invite in the cool wisdom of Air. In the south, call in the passion and enthusiasm of the Fire element. Invite in the empathy of Water in the west and complete the circle by turning back to the north.

Call on a higher power. Spells are usually activated by invoking energy from a higher power. In Wicca this may be the Goddess or God, Lord or Lady, or any other deity whose vibe matches the witch's energy or intention. You could investigate this further to see what feels right for you, or simply call on the Universe to assist you when casting your spell.

At the end of your spell, give thanks to the Universe/any deities you've asked for help and close the circle in the reverse direction.

Setting up an altar

Many witches have a dedicated space at home where they keep their magical items and cast their spells. Your altar can be as elaborate or as simple as you like. Whether you choose a shelf, a windowsill or a specific table with an altar cloth, keep the space clean and free of everyday, non-magical items. You could include candles, a small cauldron, crystals, your wand, your daily oracle card and items to represent the elements in the north, south, east and west of the space (see page 124 for more on this). You can have more than one altar, of course, or set up a temporary one in a different room or at your desk, depending on the spell you're casting.

Adapting spells

Spells use symbolism and sometimes visualization to send out your request to the universe, but they're not precise recipes. If you don't have a particular item to hand, swap it out, or if you feel that something else works better for you, use that instead. The most important thing about a spell is that it's relevant to you. The same goes for the incantations, so don't be afraid to use your own words or adapt them to your purpose.

Most importantly, though, enjoy making magic, claiming your Boss Witch power and getting the career you've not only dreamed of, but deserve.

The Boss Witch

form
1

WITCH WAY?

Decisions, decisions ... your whole career is based on them. Whether you're trying to work out the next step on your career path or choosing between a lunchtime panini or baguette, the Boss Witch has got it covered. The rituals, spells and charms in this chapter will enable you to take some time out, tune in to your intuition and weigh up your options ... and then decide to go for the hummus and feta wrap.

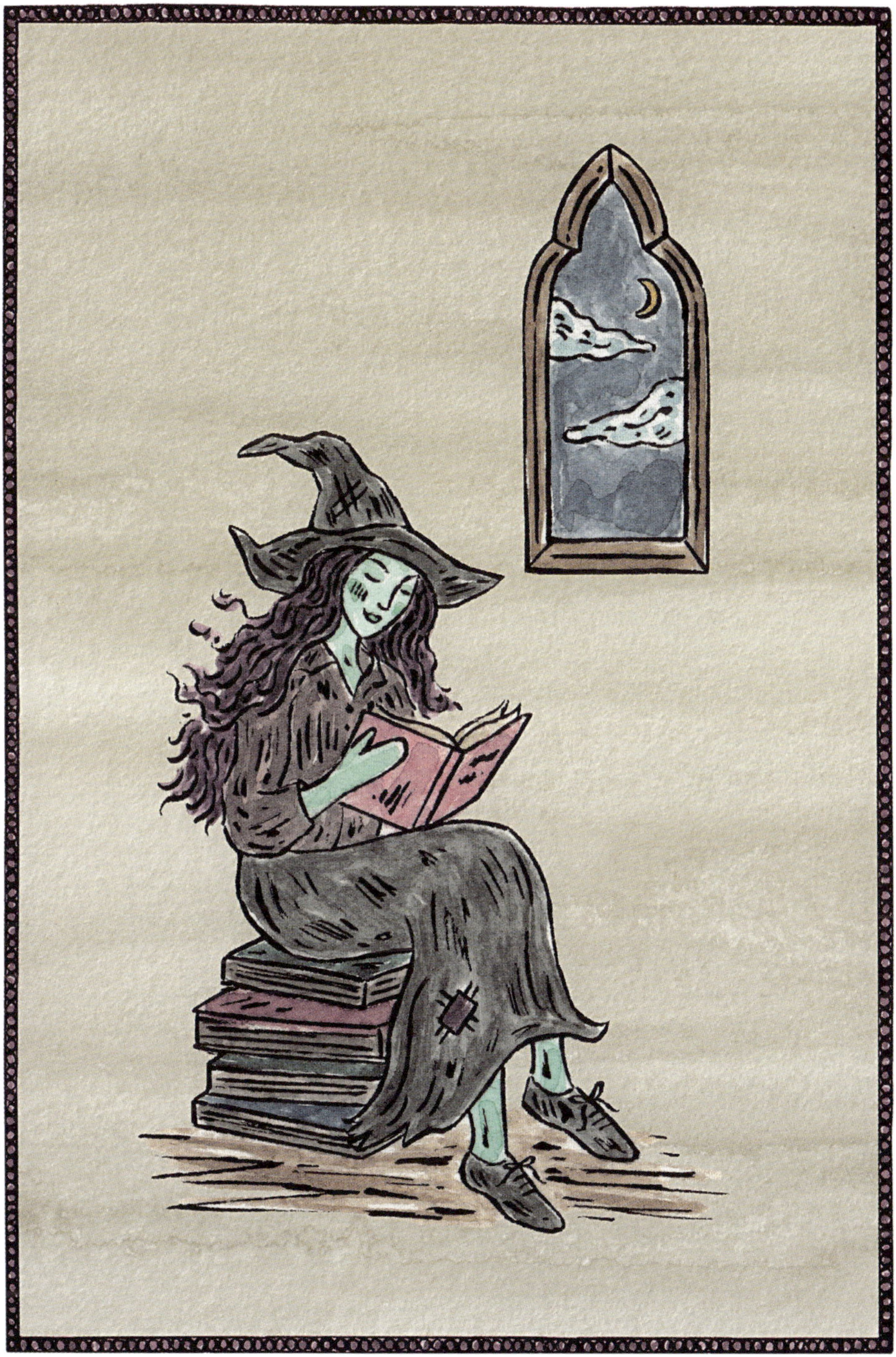

A PAPERCLIP PERSPECTIVE CHARM

If you find yourself losing sleep over making the 'wrong' choice and derailing your career forever, it's time to pause and get some perspective. While it's true that choosing your next career move might change the path of your life for a while, it's not the last decision you'll ever make.

This charm will help you to stay calm when making those big decisions. The paperclips linked together represent the steps you take on your career path, while the symbol of a circle reminds us that as the wheel of life turns, more chances and opportunities will come our way.

MATERIALS:
1 red paperclip (or a silver one bent into a slightly different shape)
11 silver paperclips

Cleanse the paperclips to dispel any dull energy they've picked up hanging around in the stationery cupboard. Then take the red one, which represents the decision you're about to make, and link a silver clip to it. Continue linking the clips together, one by one, until you have a chain. Link the final silver clip onto the first red one, and pass the chain through your hands, holding each link in turn as you recite:

I forge this chain and seal it fast,

This step I take is not my last,

I'm grounded in this peace I feel,

I make my choice, so turns the wheel

You can keep your paperclip charm under your pillow to calm your subconscious mind while you sleep, or stash it in your bag or desk drawer, and run it through your fingers in moments of stress to tap back into the sense of perspective you've conjured here.

SMOKE SCRYING

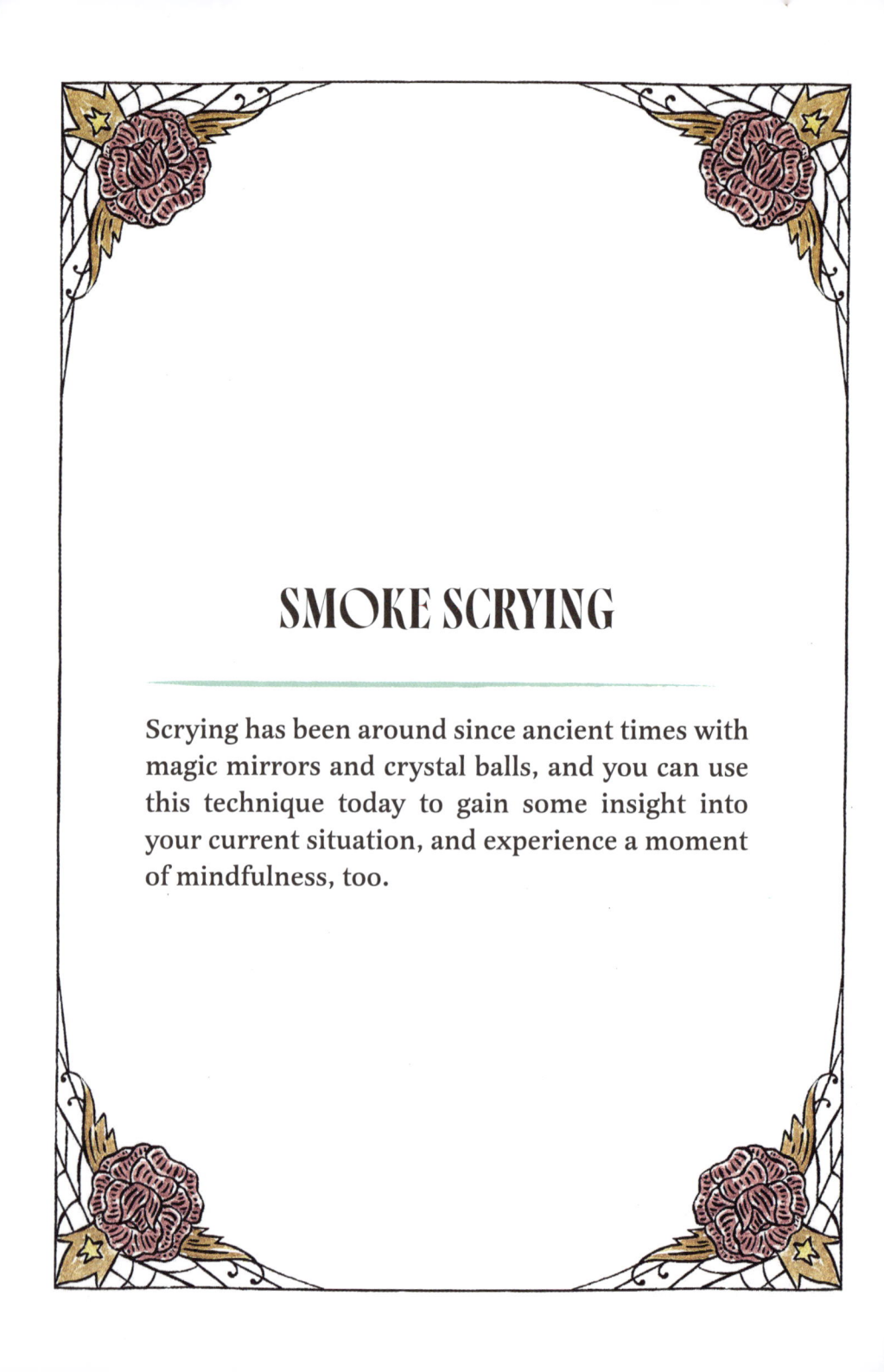

Scrying has been around since ancient times with magic mirrors and crystal balls, and you can use this technique today to gain some insight into your current situation, and experience a moment of mindfulness, too.

MATERIALS:
A stick of sandalwood incense
A journal and pen

All you really need to give scrying a go is the right mindset and something to stare at. This ritual suggests burning incense, but you could try gazing at a candle flame or raindrops tracking down your window. With a bit of practice, you'll be able to turn a trip to the water cooler into a quick scrying session, or to reflect for a while on the mirror in the bathroom.

COLOUR MAGIC

Colour magic is easy to use and, in fact, you're probably doing it already. If your phone case, shoes and hair are all red, for example, you're giving out strong, passionate energy. Different colours have different associations. You can make this work for you by intentionally choosing, say, orange nail polish for confidence when you're doing a presentation, or a green scarf when you ask your boss for a pay rise. You can also enhance your spells by choosing a candle, crystal, piece of paper or pen in a particular colour, to include these qualities into your magic. Here are some traditional colour correspondences, but if there's a different association that works for you, go with that for maximum Boss Witch power.

Yellow – happiness, friendships and optimism

Orange – creativity and career issues, confidence and enthusiasm

Red – passion, sex, strength, anger and energy

Grey – protection

Blue – communication, loyalty and calm

Indigo – intuition and serenity

Pink – love, romance and self-care

Purple – spirituality, wisdom and psychic abilities

Brown – stability, grounding and endurance

Black – to absorb negativity, protection and binding

White – clarity, peace and new beginnings

CONSULT THE ORACLE

If you haven't discovered oracle cards, it's time to start! There are hundreds of different themed packs that can offer insight into your situation and any decisions you need to make. Do some research before you choose your first pack. Pick a theme you love, whether it's trees, anime or sci-fi, and once you've got your cards, cleanse them by knocking the pack gently. Find a nice bag to store them in and use them often.

There's no need to lay out tricky spreads or commit card meanings to memory as life is complicated enough. Picking a single card at a time is a great way to get to know your oracle cards. You might like to have a ritual for this, such as lighting a white candle for clarity and reflecting on your query before picking a card from the pack. However, if you need a speedy bit of advice, just give the pack a shuffle and choose. You can also download oracle cards to your phone and swipe through the pack to make your selection, which is excellent for a bit of discreet witchery on the go.

Once you have your card, study it carefully before you turn to the guidebook. How do you feel about the image? Can you spot a link to your query? Note down any ideas, then read the card's meaning. Display the card where you can see it throughout the day; perhaps set it as your phone wallpaper or put it on your altar to reflect on. Another good option is to pick three cards: one each for the past, the present and the possible outcomes of your situation.

And remember, you're in charge of the decision making when you use oracle cards. They're a tool to shed light on your situation and subconscious feelings, but you're in control of what you do next.

QUICK-FIX DECISION-MAKING TRICKS

If you haven't got time to carry out a full ritual and you've been banned from burning incense at your desk, there are some speedy things you can do to get witchy guidance.

Coin flip

The important thing about flipping a coin isn't whether it comes up heads or tails ... it's how you feel about which way up it lands. That initial spark of excitement or disappointment is your guide. It's your subconscious speaking up, so listen to it. You could have a lucky coin, cleansed and kept for this purpose. It's even more powerful if it was minted in the year of your birth.

Go with your gut

Get in touch with your witchy intuition by tuning in to how your body feels in different situations. Try to be more aware of your signs of tension and stress (such as hunched shoulders and gritted teeth), excitement (butterflies in your stomach) and unease (a churning in your abdomen). As you become more aware of these signals, you'll become more adept at trusting your intuition.

Pendulum

Often, as a crystal on a chain or cord, a pendulum will move in one direction for 'yes' and another for 'no' and will also display a neutral 'no answer' response. Tune in to your pendulum with a few easy questions first to see how it works for you. Wearing it as a necklace will keep it charged up with your energy, plus you'll be ready for any on-the-spot decision making.

Look for signs

Do you find yourself suddenly seeing the same image cropping up on the socials, in pictures or shop windows? It could be a particular animal or an object that keeps catching your eye. Look up the symbolism of whatever your sign might be; a stag represents taking the lead, for example. The Universe is giving you a clue ...

A POST-IT POWER-WORDS SPELL

You've been in your current job for a while and everything's a bit meh. You don't want to be there forever, but what *do* you want to do? You've got approximately zero ideas about what you should apply for next.

So, what can you do about it?

To work out your next step, you need an overall destination in mind, and this spell combines brainstorming with word magic to set you off in the right direction. So, put your sticky note stash to good use and discover your career power-words.

MATERIALS:
A white candle or white sage incense
Your journal and pen
A stack of sticky notes

Light the candle or incense (for clarity) and settle down with your journal. First, reflect on where you are now, listing anything about your current job that you'd like to include in a future role. Then, think about things that you dislike and reframe them as positives to look for next time: 'I'd like to be part of a team,' rather than 'I don't want to work alone,' for example.

Now, picture yourself doing your dream job: where are you working, and who are you with? What are the hours like? Is it desk-based or are you outdoors? If you're unsure, is there anyone whose role could inspire you? What did you dream of doing as a child? Finally, list in your journal any issues you feel passionate about: the environment, social care, really, really good coffee ... note it all down.

Look through your notes and highlight six words that sum up the most important elements for you. These are your power words. Write each on a sticky note and ask aloud, 'Universe, please guide me towards a role that includes these things ... So mote it be.'

Pop the sticky notes somewhere you'll see them every morning and repeat your request every time you do. You can display them in other ways, too: written on pebbles on your altar or as a word-cloud on your desktop. And don't forget to stick the notes on your laptop every time you do a job search. You'll soon find yourself drawn in the right direction.

2

DIVINE TIMING

If you think the only people who need to worry about the full moon are werewolves (and their families), think again. The changing phases of the moon can give an added energy to your spellcasting if you work in tune with them, and this is also true for the days of the week. The most important factor in Boss Witchery is always your intention, but, like sriracha sauce on a taco, synchronizing your magic with the stars and planets can give it an extra kick. In this chapter we will discover spells and rituals where it's all in the timing.

Book of Common Spells
Spell Bound
WAND
HEX VII
HECATES HOME
Cauldron Stews
Macbeth

MOON MAGIC

It takes just over 29 days for the moon to go through a complete cycle, which is roughly the same length of time as the average menstrual cycle. Many women feel a resonance between the phases of the moon and the changes they experience throughout the month. Living in tune with the lunar phases and casting spells accordingly carries extra feminine energy. There are some great apps you can use to keep track of the moon, and it's worth noting how the different stages affect you, as it may come in handy when timing work or any other activities.

New moon
A great time for new beginnings, job hunting and starting new projects. Cast a spell now to set any intentions for the month and work on them as the moon waxes. It can take several cycles to manifest results, but you should see a change by the next new moon. Try An Invitation to Inspiration, page 28; An All-Out Spell to Get That Job, page 40.

Waxing moon

As the moon grows, this is a time to develop positive relationships at work and cast spells for prosperity, including increased wealth. Try A Candle Spell for Team Harmony, page 82; 'Pay Rise, Please!' Money-Drawing Oil, page 102.

Full moon

The moon is at maximum power, and you should see the results of your efforts. You can also cast spells that need an extra energy boost now. It's a great time for prophecy, too. Try Consult the Oracle, page 16.

Waning moon

As the light of the moon begins to decrease, cast banishing spells or spells to remove negativity from your work life. Try A Ritual for Moving On from Rejection, page 136; Cord-Cutting After an Office Romance, page 128.

Dark moon

This is when the last, slimmest crescent of the waning moon is visible in the sky, just before the new moon. You may feel drained, so be sure to clock off on time, rest up and reflect. Try A Dark Moon Ritual, page 26.

A DARK MOON RITUAL

Even Boss Witches need to recharge now and then, so carry out this ritual every month on the night of the dark moon. This is the moment when one moon cycle blends into the next, so it's the perfect time to release any worries from the previous few weeks, before starting any shiny new projects in the weeks ahead.

MATERIALS:
A toothpick or pin
A black candle
A muslin bag containing a bay leaf,
   plus a good pinch of any of the following: cloves (for banishing), rosemary (for healing), basil (for protection) and sage (for cleansing)
A white candle
A clear quartz crystal
A handful of Himalayan salt or sea salt (for cleansing)
Some slices of lemon

Before you draw your bath, give the tub a quick clean. Reflect on anything negative from the last month at work, then, with the toothpick, inscribe something that symbolizes this at the top of the black candle. If you use the poop emoji to represent your manager, that's your call; Boss Witches don't judge!

Draw your bath, attaching the bag of herbs to the tap so that the water runs through it. Say, 'I leave behind all that does not benefit me,' and light the candle, placing it on the side of the bath. Place your white candle here too. Add the crystal, the salt and lemon to the water, and stir the water with your hand in a clockwise motion. Visualize the cleansing power of these natural ingredients mixing, then say, 'I soak away my stress,' as you lower yourself into the tub.

Focus on the candle flame. When you feel relaxed and your symbol has burned away, light the white candle with the flame from the black one, saying, 'I welcome a fresh start and new beginnings.' Extinguish the black candle and relax back into the water.

Hold the quartz crystal and charge it up by visualizing pure white energy coming from the white candle into the crystal, and into you. Carry the crystal in your bag or keep it on your desk during the month ahead.

NOTE: If you don't have a bathtub, you can change this ritual and carry out a foot-soak in a bowl, instead.

AN INVITATION TO INSPIRATION

You've cleaned your desktop or laptop, alphabetized everything in the stationery cupboard and made everyone a coffee but you can't put it off any longer ... It's zero hour: time to start that new report/project/artwork, but your mind is as blank as your computer screen and you need some inspiration!

So, what can you do about it?

Hit the fruit bowl! Orange is the colour of creativity, and there's an easy way you can tap into its energy ... by eating one. This spell works well if carried out at the new moon. The full spell involves some candle magic and is best done at home if you don't want to set off the office sprinkler system. However, there's also a quick-fix version you can do at your desk.

MATERIALS:
An orange and a knife
A bay leaf
A small orange candle
A pen
Twine

If you're working the spell at home, cleanse your altar then hold the orange in both hands and focus on its colour. Visualize a stream of bright orange energy flowing from the fruit, down your arms and into your mind and body.

Cut the orange in half, setting one piece in the centre of your altar, cut-side up. Now, take the bay leaf and draw Kenaz, the creativity rune on it.

Attach the bay leaf to the candle with the twine, then stand the candle in the orange-half by pushing it into the flesh. Make sure it is not likely to tip over. Light the candle, reciting:

I call in creativity –

Inspiration flows through me,

I give thanks for this energy,

So, mote it be

Kenaz Rune

Your spell will be activated as the bay leaf burns. Eat the other half of the orange to absorb its zesty power.

At-your-desk option:
Draw the creativity rune on a sticky note and stick this to your computer/tablet screen. Focus on it as you eat an orange/tangerine, feeling clarity and creativity flow through you. If an orange is too messy, you could sip eucalyptus or peppermint tea. Eucalyptus is great for clearing creative blockages, and peppermint peps up your productivity.

MORE TIMING TIPS

It's not just the phase of the moon that can enhance your magic. Here are some other ways to add some extra spice to your spellcasting.

Days of the week
Each day of the week is ruled by a celestial body that makes it suitable for particular types of spellwork.

SUNDAY: ruled by the sun, bright and bold. Cast your most ambitious spells today to summon wealth, promotion and new beginnings.

MONDAY: ruled by the moon, which governs our thoughts and feelings. A good time for scrying, relaxing and reflecting on your innermost desires.

TUESDAY: ruled by Mars, the god of war. A good day for protective spells, or hexing.

WEDNESDAY: ruled by Mercury, speedy messenger and trickster. Cast spells involving travel, luck and money ... or subterfuge!

THURSDAY: ruled by Jupiter, who symbolizes power, making this a good time to conjure a promotion or carry out spells involving justice.

FRIDAY: ruled by Venus, who represents love (of course!). If you're looking to nurture positive relationships at work, today's the day to work those magics.

SATURDAY: ruled by Saturn and linked to death and endings. Now's the time to cut unhealthy ties and bind anyone who is spreading negativity in the office.

Seasons
Many witches celebrate festivals that tie into the turning of the seasons, and this can benefit your spells, too. For Pagans the year ends at Samhain (31 October/Halloween) with a new year beginning on 1 November. You can cast spells to help you shed things you no longer need in the autumn, plant the seeds for new projects at new year and then conjure them into bloom with the first signs of life as winter turns into spring.

A 'TAKE BACK YOUR TIME' SPELL

Time pressure is one of the main sources of stress at work. If you find yourself so worried about hitting deadlines that 'inventing a time machine' has made it onto your to-do list, you might need to have a rethink about your schedule. This spell is great for identifying and removing the timewasters in your life.

MATERIALS:
A sticky note
A pen
Correction fluid
Scissors

You can carry out this spell whenever you feel your time is being wasted, during a needlessly long phone call, for example, or just when you look back on your week and realize there is a task or person that's regularly wasting your precious time.

Write the name of the time-wasting person or activity on the sticky note. Then draw a cross over each letter, and correction fluid over the crossed-out letters one by one, saying:

My day is precious,

You waste my time,

I banish you,

And claim what's mine

Finally, fold the sticky note several times into a thin strip, making sure you fold it away from yourself each time, before snipping it into small pieces and placing them in the bin.

NOTE: If you find you're constantly weighed down by your workload and you've asked for support but received none, it may be time to take your Boss Witch marvellousness elsewhere. Life is too short to spend your entire day drowning in work.

QUICK-FIX TIMING TRICKS

You may carry it with you all the time to stay connected with your friends/colleagues/pets, but your phone is also a powerful tool for witchery, too. Here are some ways to use your tech to help with timing spells.

Your phone

Set a reminder:
Create a daily alert reminding you of an intention you've set for the month. If you're working towards a pay rise, you could set an alert to say, 'I deserve more money,' to keep your spell on track.

Apps:
Stay in tune with the moon and time your spells to perfection with an app that tells you the current moon phase. There are apps that detail the planetary influences and astrological info, too.

Lockscreen:
You look at your lockscreen dozens of times a day, so it's an excellent place to put an empowering image: create a sigil (a personalized magical symbol, see page 42) linked to your job search, use a picture that reminds you of your intentions, or a photo that connects you with your past self in a moment when you felt powerful and happy.

Notes:
Keep a note of your intentions or power words or use notes for spells then, at the new moon, create a note with emojis to symbolize what you want to manifest. Check back at the full moon to see how you're progressing.

Your laptop/desktop computer

Use a powerful word as your log-in for a daily boost or set your wallpaper to match the changing seasons or moon phases.

Your smart speaker

Brilliant for setting up a 'routine': when you say hello in the morning, set your speaker to reply with a personalized affirmation, read your horoscope, play a mood-boosting song or meditation, or read aloud anything you've scheduled into your diary ... Try scheduling in 'I am working towards my career goals,' every day, and your speaker will remind you.

3

WITCHES GET PROMOTED

I know you're brilliant. You know you're brilliant. And everyone else would know you're brilliant, too, if only you could get your voice heard or your CV to the top of the pile. Well, with a little Boss Witch magic, you can add some sparkle to your applications and ensure you stand out from the crowd. Whether you're pitching an idea, going for a promotion or attending a group interview, there's plenty you can do to give your efforts a (witch)crafty boost.

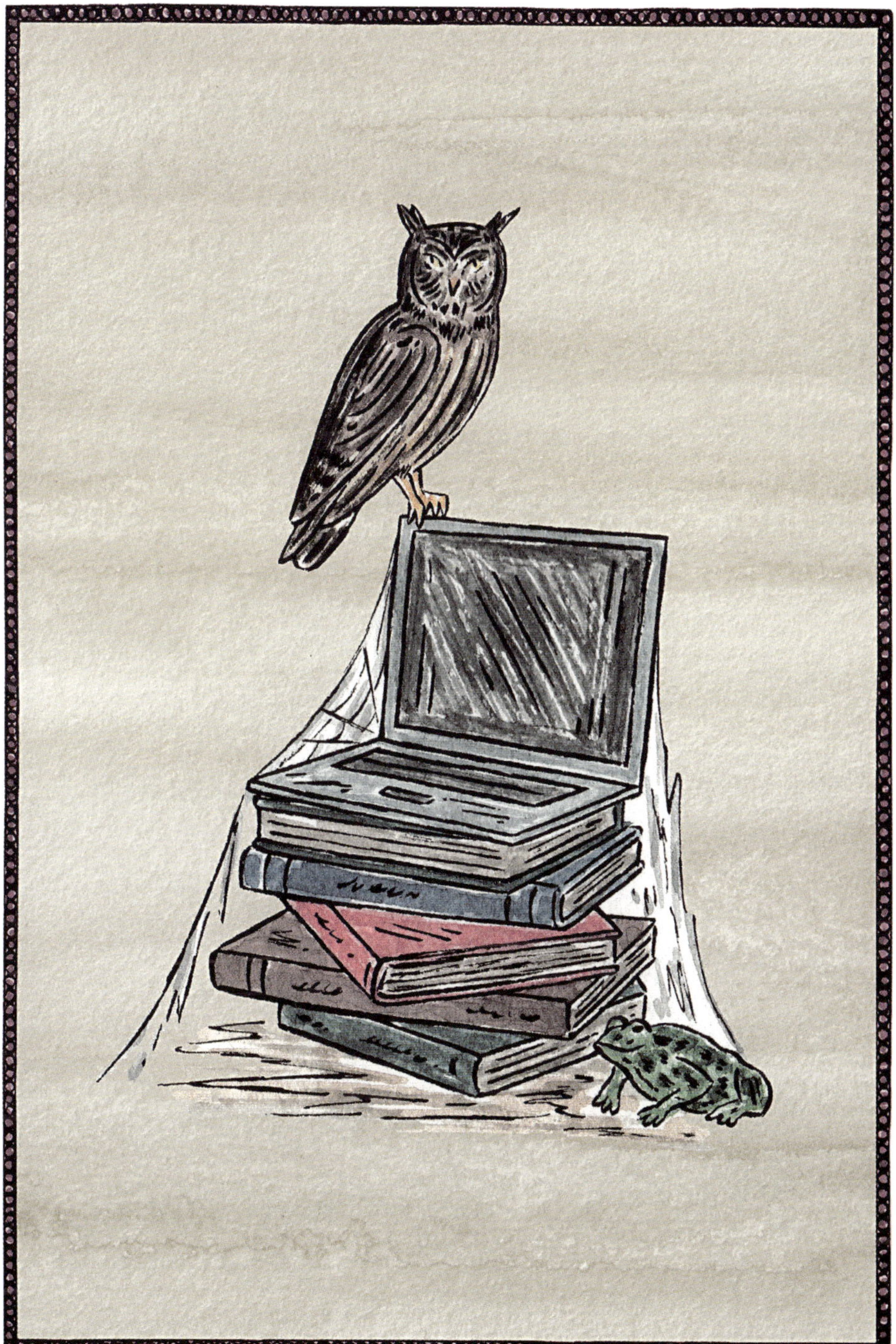

A LIPSTICK SPELL FOR CONFIDENCE

Even the most confident of us can experience imposter syndrome the night before a big meeting or presentation, but that needn't be the case with this simple spell. Use it for an empowering boost to go and smash it.

There are two parts to the spell: a ritual to charge up your confidence the night before, followed by a quick fix to unleash its full power the next day.

MATERIALS:
An orange or red candle (for courage and strength)
A candleholder
Your favourite lipstick, gloss or balm
A slip of paper and a pen

Perform this spell before bed, once you've set aside all the practicalities of the day. Take a relaxing, cleansing bath, then gather your supplies and get ready for some Boss Witchery.

Light the candle on your altar and spend a few moments staring into the flame. Take some slow, deep breaths and think about the challenge you're preparing for.

Next, set your intention: write, 'I am confident,' on your slip of paper in bold letters. Focus on this as you pick up the lipstick. Picture yourself at your meeting or presentation full of poise and confidence. Let this feeling flow down through your hands and into the lipstick. Circle the candle flame (with the lipstick at a safe distance) three times in a clockwise direction to charge it with fiery energy.

Apply the lipstick and say, 'I am confident,' three times, before kissing the piece of paper to seal your spell. Fold it and leave it beneath the lipstick overnight. Don't forget to blow out the candle!

In the morning, pop your lipstick in your bag and tuck the piece of paper into a pocket, your phone case or even your bra; anything goes when witching under the radar. Before you enter the meeting room, pause, apply the lipstick and reconjure that feeling of confidence. Then walk in with your head held high: you'll be brilliant.

AN ALL-OUT SPELL TO GET THAT JOB

You're applying for so many jobs you need to hire someone to keep track of them all, but you're either getting turned down (rude) or getting no response at all (also rude). It's time to go all out with this powerful spell to get your application noticed … and to get you that job.

So, what can you do about it?

Focusing all your efforts on a few choice applications, rather than a mass of different jobs, is a good approach. Next time you find a role that really appeals to you, send off the best application you can, and then carry out this spell to blast your energy and enthusiasm into the Universe after it.

The spell uses quite a few components because we're going all out here! However, you can ad lib if you need to. The yellow candle, crystal and image of the sun all attract success, while the coffee and burning of your wish will make things happen more speedily.

MATERIALS:
Your favourite music
A yellow candle
A slip of paper and pen
A bay leaf
A pinch each of dried basil,
    cinnamon powder and coffee
    powder
Your cauldron
A jar or pot with a lid
An image of the sun or the Sun tarot card
A citrine crystal

Start this spell by cleansing yourself and your surroundings with some uplifting music. Pick your favourite song, the livelier the better, and sing along and dance to get rid of any negative energy.

Now, it's time to focus (and recover from the dancing): light the candle and take some calming breaths. Stare into the flame and think about the job you've applied for. What do you like about it? Can you picture yourself in the role?

Next, write down at least three positive affirmations, such as, 'I love my new job,' 'I feel financially secure,' or 'I am enjoying working with my new team,' whatever is important to you about the role. Remember to use the present tense, as if you've already been successful.

Add the bay leaf, basil, cinnamon and coffee to your cauldron. Now fold the paper three times towards you, and set it alight in the candle flame. Put the paper into your cauldron and let it burn along with the herbs.

Once the ashes are cool, pop them in the jar or pot, close it and place it on your altar on top of the image of the sun and alongside the citrine crystal.

Every morning, give the jar a shake to re-energize your spell. If you don't hear anything after a week, send a polite and concise follow-up email to show your boss-to-be that you're enthusiastic and the right witch for the job!

WITCHES GET PROMOTED

SIGILS FOR SUCCESS

These sassy little symbols can help you manifest everything from strong boundaries to a promotion. They're easy to create and activate, and all you need is a pen and a piece of paper.

Start by writing down a simple, specific statement of your intent, for example, 'Better communication.' Don't make it too long, or it'll be tricky to create your sigil. Now cross out any vowels and repeated letters. For our example, you'll be left with: btrcmn. Combine the remaining letters to create a symbol and be as creative as you like. You could try superimposing them, reversing them or drawing them upside-down.

Once you have your sigil, draw it a few times, focusing on your intention, and then activate it. A simple way to do this is to burn it, but you could carve it into a piece of food and eat it, or 'write' it on the ground with water and let it evaporate.

You can keep your sigil on a sticky note in your phone case or on your desk, or draw it on the bathroom mirror every morning or in the air with a wand or pen before you start work. A sigil also works well as a discreet temporary tattoo, doodled on your wrist.

You can include them in other spells, too. A simple CV spell is to create an 'Employ me' sigil and trace it with a finger on your CV on your computer screen before you send off a job application.

Don't forget, you need to follow your sigil up with actions, too, to achieve your goal. You can't just create a sigil for 'Become CEO' and sit back and watch Netflix while you wait for it to happen, unfortunately!

Sigils are powerful charms, and by using them instead of words to capture your intention, you're working on a deeper level as they unlock the power of your unconscious mind.

WITCHES GET PROMOTED

A 'PICK ME' TALISMAN

If you're pitching an idea or attending a group interview, you need to stand out from the competition. This talisman will ensure your true Boss Witch colours shine through. A talisman can be any small meaningful object that you charge up with your intention and then wear to attract whatever it is you desire.

MATERIALS:
A small pebble, shell or crystal (see below)
A slip of paper and a pen
Some moon water (see below)
Some cord
A small pouch

As this charm is all about standing out from the crowd, choose a small pebble, shell or crystal that draws your attention to be the base of your talisman; a hag stone (a pebble with a hole in it) would be perfect, as you can easily hang this on a cord to wear.

Write your intention down on the slip of paper: 'Pick me for the promotion!', for example. Place this on your altar along with your stone and meditate on it every day for a week to charge up your talisman.

Spritz your talisman with moon water to seal it. Moon water is water that has been left in a bowl in the light of the full moon and then decanted into a small spray bottle. If you've chosen a hag stone, thread it onto the piece of cord, otherwise put your talisman in the pouch and close it up with the cord, knotting it three times.

Wear your talisman to ensure others are drawn to your Boss Witchery. Don't forget to charge it up regularly.

NOTE: This talisman can help you stand out so you're not passed over for promotion ... but be honest with yourself if this happens to you regularly. If you're not enthusiastic about your job, you might be giving out a message that a talisman can't change. Maybe it's time to find a different role, where you can shine.

CRYSTAL POWER

Many witches like to work with crystals, harnessing their different properties. Crystals can be charged with energy to help manifest something specific ... plus they're sparkly natural wonders, and an easy way to bring magic to your workplace without anyone asking too many questions. Who's to know that the little carved rose quartz cat on the end of your desk is actually there to promote a better relationship with your tricky office neighbour?

But which crystal should you pick? Stand in front of a display of tumbled crystals and you'll be drawn to whichever you need the most. Here are the properties of just a few of them.

Amethyst
for healing and moving on from any difficult work moments

Moonstone
for enhancing psychic abilities when planning ahead

Citrine
to spark creativity when you're starting a new project

Onyx
for strength (perfect for that three-hour weekly progress meeting)

Obsidian
to release emotions and shield against negativity

Haematite
for grounding during a stressy one-to-one

Quartz
a powerful healer and good go-to for any situation

Rose quartz
for enhancing relationships and self-care

Tiger's eye
for repelling work-based negativity

Turquoise
for good luck and to soothe you in stressful situations

Jade
to attract good luck in an interview

You can carry crystals with you, wear them as jewellery, have them in your workspace or hold one to meditate with.

Crystals should always be cleansed and charged before use. Cleanse with salt, incense or water, but check that your crystal won't be damaged by water first. Charge them up by leaving them in sunlight or moonlight.

A TECH SPELL FOR TALKING THE TALK

Do you find it tricky talking about yourself? A good old gossip in the kitchen about what you did at the weekend is easy enough, but what about when you're asked to outline your skills and experience? Speaking confidently under pressure can be a challenge, but this ritual will help you to get it right.

MATERIALS:
A mirror, camera, or something to focus on
A printout of your CV
A cup of peppermint tea
Your phone

First, find a place where you can talk to yourself without alarming your colleagues, flatmates or pets. Set up the mirror or camera in front of you, or choose something to focus on when you speak – you could aim your words at an object, plant or even a pet! Make sure you have your CV and tea to hand. Now, switch on the torch on your phone and use the light to cast a circle in a clockwise direction around you, saying:

I cast this light to set my space,

Help me to practise in this place

Switch off the torch and look over your CV. Now practise talking through it, as if someone has asked you 'To tell them about …' each section. Speaking aloud is very different from reading something through in your head, and in witchcraft, spoken words take on an extra power.

Don't try to memorize perfect answers. This ritual is all about getting comfortable with talking about yourself, after all. You're not learning lines for a play, so vary your answers each time. Sip the tea as you practise; peppermint aids clear communication.

When you've finished, close the circle, moving your phone torch anticlockwise around you as you say:

I spoke my truth, my meaning clear

With thanks, I end my practice here.

2

VERY IMPORTANT WITCH

As a VIW, you have go-to rituals to deal with stress, you're listened to with respect whenever you offer up your ideas, and you kicked imposter syndrome in the proverbials ages ago, right? Right?! Well, just in case you haven't ticked all these things off your to-do list yet, here is some Boss Witch magic to take care of any stragglers. And if you're after a smoother commute, or some cunning spells that will never get spotted in the workplace, we've got that covered, too.

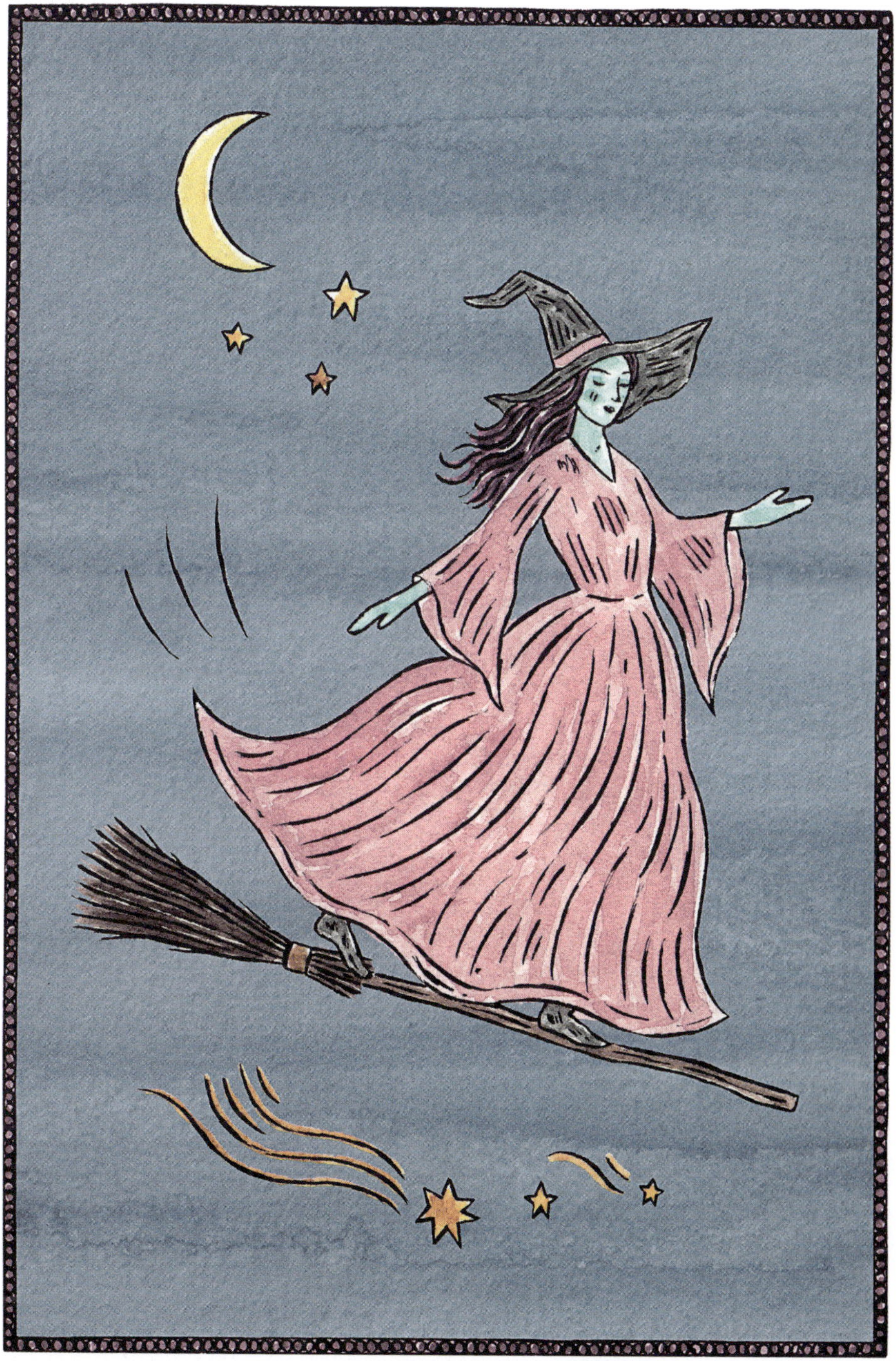

'HOCUS-POCUS, CALM AND FOCUS' BALM

Your workday is a blur of back-to-back appointments, and it can be hard to show up like a Boss Witch for each one. There's never time for a proper break, but you need an easy way to reset before rushing to the next meeting.

So, what can you do about it?

This calm balm is the perfect mini-recharge ritual to apply between appointments, giving you a moment to pause and focus. Lavender has calming properties, while camomile is good for balancing your emotions. You could buy a ready-made balm, but it's fun to make one yourself, and you can imbue the ingredients with your intentions as you make it. It's also a chance to let loose with the witchery, combining herbs, tweaking ingredients and stirring everything in your cauldron (read: saucepan).

MATERIALS:
125 ml (4 fl oz/1/2 cup) olive oil
60 ml (2 fl oz/1/4 cup) dried herb mix (camomile and lavender work well)
2 tablespoons beeswax (or carnauba wax)
2 saucepans
A large glass jar
A wooden chopstick or spoon
3 tablespoons coconut oil
A few drops of vitamin E oil
10 drops lavender oil
10 drops patchouli oil
A tea towel or strainer
Some small pots with secure lids

Start by infusing the olive oil with the herbs. Warm the oil in the saucepan, then stir in the mixture over a very low heat. It will take an hour for this to infuse. Stir in a clockwise direction every now and then, sending calming vibes into the mix. If you have time, you can make a larger quantity by adding herbs to a kilner jar, filling with olive oil and leaving them to steep for at least a month. Strain the oil and discard the herby residue.

Add the beeswax to the jar and place in a clean saucepan containing an inch or so of simmering water. When the beeswax has started to melt, add the olive oil to the jar, giving it another stir and a blast of your witchy vibes. Add in the coconut oil and vitamin E, which will act as a preservative.

Once everything has melted, remove the jar from the heat and allow it to cool for a few minutes. Finally add the lavender essential oil, followed by the patchouli (great for grounding), stirring as you say:

Relax and ground me with this balm,

Help me to focus, keep me calm

Pour the balm into the pots (or use a clean jar) and make time to apply, or at least sniff, regularly on your busiest workdays.

QUICK-FIX TRAVEL TRICKS

Whether it's the daily commute, a flight or a quick dash to the shops for more printer ink, travelling can be a pain. Here are some simple ways to use magic to improve your journeys.

MATERIALS:
A small cotton bag
A handful of dried comfrey leaves
A handful of dried lavender flowers
1 whole nutmeg
A small piece of malachite or amethyst

Travel pass sigil

Create a sigil for 'Safe and speedy travel' (see page 42) and keep this with your travel pass or in your phone case, if you keep your pass on your phone.

A come-home stone

Choose a small stone from your garden or an area near your home and anoint it with comfrey leaves before you leave home, saying:

To guard me on my journey

I power up this stone,

Protect me on my travels

And bring me safely home

A safe-travel pouch

If you're feeling stitch-crafty, as well as witch-crafty, you could embroider a safe travel sigil on the outside of the bag before you fill it. Place the items in the bag, holding each for a moment in your hands and visualizing a smooth and speedy journey as you add it. All of these things are traditionally associated with safe travel. Seal the pouch with three secure knots and keep it in your bag or car to protect you while you're away.

A POWER CORD TO BANISH IMPOSTER SYNDROME

If you experience imposter syndrome, you are not alone. It rears its head when we are plagued with self-doubt, rather than acknowledging our brilliant achievements. This spell will set the balance right.

MATERIALS:
Laptop/phone/paper and pen
Citrus incense
A variety of crystal or other decorative beads
Three lengths of thick cord or ribbon

This spell has two stages. The first is to build up a record of your achievements, over the weeks during a waxing moon. Write down all the things you're most proud of, from always acing your times-tables tests as a baby witch to defeating that ogre who tried to take credit for your ideas last week.

For the second part of the spell, when the moon is full, look through everything you've written and then send yourself an email summarizing your greatest hits. I know this might feel a bit icky, but it's good practice for receiving glowing feedback. I'll start you off: 'Dear XXX, You're amazing! This month alone, you have …' Once you're happy with your message, press send as you say, 'I achieved all this!'

Next, light the incense and open your email from you to you. Read it through and pick out your biggest achievements, then choose a bead to represent each one. Knot the three cords together at one end and begin to plait them. After a few centimetres, take the first bead and slide it onto one of the cords, visualizing the achievement it represents and remembering how you felt at the time, saying, 'I achieved this.' Continue plaiting for another few centimetres, repeating the process for the rest of the beads. Finish your power cord with a sturdy knot and keep it with you. If you feel imposter syndrome again, touch each bead in turn to remind yourself of what a wonderful witch you are.

'HEAR ME!' POTION

Drinking a potion is a great way of supercharging yourself with magical energy, and there's nothing more witchy than stirring a bubbling cauldron. This delicious punch will soothe your throat chakra and help you to get your voice heard. Take some to work in a flask, hot or cold, for an instant witchy hit.

INGREDIENTS:

1 bottle of ginger beer
A saucepan
A good glug of red grape juice
A small glug of blackcurrant squash
Ginger (for success)
Slices of apple (for knowledge) and orange (for positivity)
A cinnamon stick (for power)
A bay leaf (for courage to speak your truth)
Honey (to sweeten your words)

Set the ginger beer to warm in the pan and pour in the grape juice and squash (it tastes yummy, I promise!). When everything comes to a simmer, add in the dry ingredients, holding each in turn for a moment and focusing on the qualities it will bring to your potion. You might like to acknowledge each one aloud as you add it in, saying, 'I ask for success in speaking my truth,' for example, as you add the ginger.

Now, add the honey. I like to draw a pentacle with the honey as I squeeze it in for a final witchy blessing. Starting at the top, draw a five-pointed star, followed by a clockwise circle around the edge of the pan, saying:

Bring strength to my words

With this magic brew,

Mix power with wisdom

To help me speak true

To make this into a boozy punch for a party, scale up the quantities and perhaps substitute a Malbec for the grape juice and use alcoholic ginger beer ... If you do this, chances are everyone will be speaking their truth loud and clear by the end of the evening, so use with caution!

A SALT BOWL DE-STRESSING RITUAL

It's been a hectic day, and you want nothing more than to kick off your shoes and relax, but your mind keeps replaying the day's stressful moments, and it feels like you're in an episode of *American Horror Story*.

So, what can you do about it?

A relaxing home-from-work ritual is the answer. This one takes your work lanyard/pass as a focal point and taps into the cleansing power of salt to help you de-stress.

MATERIALS:
A china bowl (wooden bowls can be spoiled by the salt)
Coarse salt: Himalayan rock salt, black salt or salt flakes all work well
A handful of peppercorns
Some sprigs of fresh rosemary, or a sprinkling of the dried herb
An essential oil of your choice
Your work pass or lanyard
A candle
A small brass bell

Create your salt bowl by adding the peppercorns and rosemary (for protection) to the salt, along with a few drops of essential oil. Mix everything around with your fingers, saying, 'May this mix absorb my stress and leave me feeling calm.' Set the bowl on your altar.

Every day, include your salt bowl as part of a wind-down ritual. For example, put away your shoes, coat and bag, and pop your lanyard on your altar, next to the salt bowl. You may want to give it a quick wipe to clean it first. If you usually have a shower, you could do that, then light a candle on your altar and stare into the flame to relax.

Press your fingers into the salt and say, 'I banish the negativity and stress from my day.' Let any stress or tension flow out of you and into the bowl. Gently ring the bell above the salt bowl to freshen it, then place your work pass on top of it, and leave it overnight, for a clean start in the morning.

Use your bowl for as long as it feels fresh, then dispose of the salt safely in the bin.

NOTE: Keep your bowl out of reach of pets as they'll get ill if they lick the salt.

UNDER-THE-RADAR GLAMOUR SPELLS

Glamour magic is an easy way to feel more powerful, and no one needs to know a thing about it. By incorporating colour magic in your clothes choices or adding intention to your make-up ritual, you can weave some under-the-radar magic to give you a boost. Also, it's much more subtle than bringing your frog familiar to work. Here are some easy ideas.

Braiding
If your hair's long enough to braid, repeat a relevant mantra as you plait: 'I am efficient and get everything done,' for example. This is a form of knot magic.

Choose your colour
Pick a colour that matches your intention (see page 14) for your make-up or clothes, or base your outfit on a favourite oracle card or image of a deity. You don't need to go full-on druid robe; a single accessory or general theme will do!

Nails
As with the clothes you wear, you can use a specific colour on your nails, or include a symbol in your nail art.

Jewellery
If it's allowed at work, this is a brilliant way to get Boss Witching because you can include specific crystals in your jewellery, wear an amulet, talisman or small spell bottle around your neck; use knot magic to create a spell bracelet; create your own jewellery from found natural items ... there's no limit!

Perfumes/scents
Choose a blend that incorporates significant scents (see page 70). You can create a ritual for applying your perfume and visualize yourself being 'powered up' as you apply it.

Beauty regime
Take moon water (see page 45) in a small spray bottle and spritz yourself to clear negative energies. Create a salt scrub to cleanse negativity before a gnarly day, or an elixir to absorb the qualities of a specific crystal.

Henna
A henna tattoo of a particular symbol, drawn with intention, is another great way of incorporating magical energy in your day.

BUILD YOUR OWN SPELL BAG

Spell bags are neat little personalized charms that are easy to make. Use your intuition to gather items that symbolize your intentions, pop them in the bag and charge them up with some meditation and visualization. Choose or make a small bag in a colour that works for your spell (see page 14). Keep it in your bag, pocket, car or a drawer at work, and wait for your charm to manifest its magic.

Here are some ideas of what to include, and what they might symbolize for you:

Natural items:

Acorns or seeds (potential and growth)

Sycamore keys (movement and progress)

Leaves (good for writing on; plus oak leaves symbolize strength)

Shells (security)

Stones (solid grounding)

Feathers (perspective and flying high)

Symbols:

A rune, sigil, symbol or sentence to sum up your intent (write it on a leaf, pebble, piece of paper, etc.)

Crystals

(See page 46)

A pinch of herbs or spice

(See page 70)

Other ideas:

Coins, rice or dried beans (wealth)

Salt (protection)

Any small charm or trinket that represents your wish

5

WITCHES WHO LUNCH

It's lunchtime! Do you: a) keep on working through your break with a soggy sandwich as your only companion, or b) take some time away from your desk/workbench/customer-interaction point and add some extra Boss Witch magic to your day? The answer's 'b', of course, so try out a grounding ritual, snack on something magical or power up ready to tackle your to-do list.

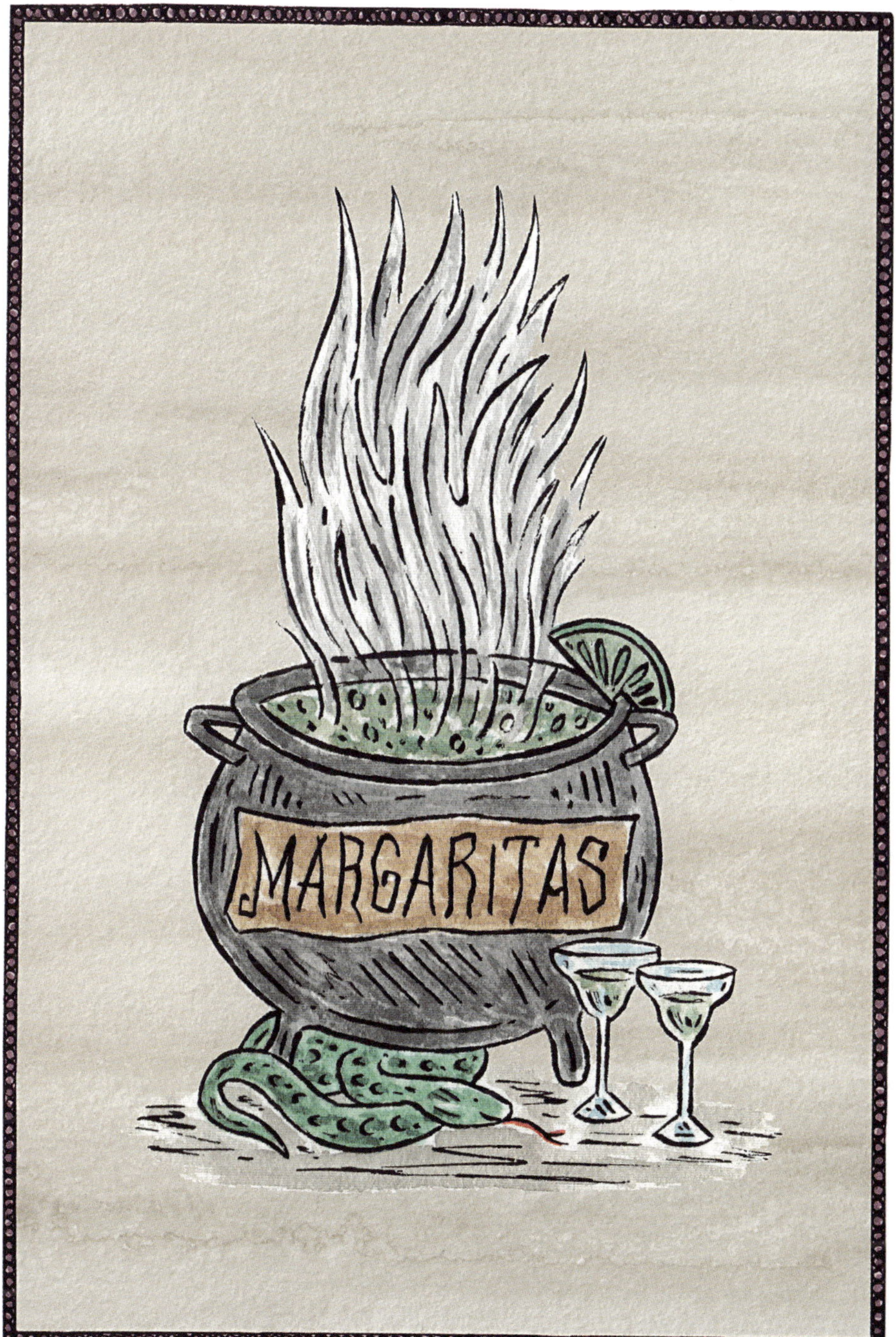
MARGARITAS

A BALANCING BREW

We all love a cuppa, but did you know that you can turn a tea break into a ritual to balance and ground you? You can do this with any hot drink, but breaking out the herbal teabags will give you the chance to incorporate a little kitchen witchery into your ritual, too.

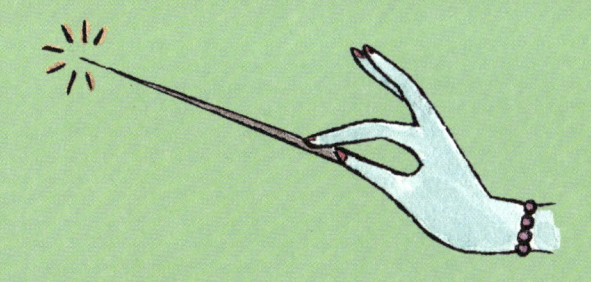

MATERIALS:
A china mug
A kettle
Your tea of choice (see page 70 for the powers of different herbs)

Many pagans work with four main elements when using magic; these are Earth, Air, Fire and Water, in case you haven't got to know them yet. They relate to many different things, including personality traits and behaviours, and keeping them in balance is usually beneficial. For example, if you lose your temper, the Fire element is dominant, and you may want to balance it with Earth by grounding yourself. A tea ritual offers us the chance to tend to each of the elements in turn, so …

Make your cuppa and settle down somewhere quiet. Release thoughts of your morning's work as you focus on your soothing brew.

Now, concentrate on your china mug, remembering that it's a material that's a gift from the Earth. Feel its weight and let this ground you, strengthening your connection with the planet beneath your feet.

Next, look at the steam coming from your drink, studying the patterns it makes before you. Breathe in the scent of your tea and let the element of Air clear your head and calm your thoughts.

Cup your drink in both hands and feel its warmth flow through you, as Fire recharges your energy and reignites your creativity and enthusiasm.

Finally, sip your drink and feel the healing power of Water balancing your emotions and nurturing your intuition. Consider the qualities of whichever herb you selected for your brew, too.

Finish your drink and return to work feeling grounded, invigorated and ready for anything!

KITCHEN WITCHIN'

There are endless ways to include the power of herbs and spices in your witchcraft. You can add them to your meals, a spell bag or a bath; scatter them for protection or use them to dress a candle or brew a cuppa … Just take your pick from the store cupboard.

Allspice for prosperity, love and luck

Basil for psychic ability and peace

Bay for success. The leaves are also handy to write a wish on

Camomile to calm and heal

Cinnamon for money, attraction and to spice up a spell

Cloves for protection and divination

Dill to counter hexes

Ginger to boost a love, money or luck spell

Lemon balm for business success and fertility

Nettle for courage and justice

Nutmeg for happiness, love and money

Pepper for banishing spells and security

Peppermint to perk up your energy and bring luck

Parsley for strength and purification

Rosemary for protection and wisdom

Sage for purification and clarity

Thyme for protection and healing

QUICK-FIX ENERGY TRICKS

We've all experienced the afternoon slump: a natural dip in energy levels that means most of us would prefer a little nap under our desk to an afternoon of ... well ... anything else. But don't worry, here are some witchy (and not-so-witchy) ways to boost your energy and make your afternoon a powerhouse of productivity.

Experience the elements
Artificial lighting messes with melatonin levels, but a burst of natural light will boost your energy. Take your lunch outside if you can, or at least near a window where you can see the world beyond your desk. This is a chance to focus on the four elements and balance yourself, so notice Earth, Water, Air and Fire (warmth) while you're outside, for extra witchy points. Take a few deep breaths to boost your oxygen levels and wake yourself up.

Pick a potion
Have a balancing brew (see page 68). Peppermint tea is great for pepping up your energy levels. Stir in a clockwise direction and visualize its healing power flowing through your body as you drink.

Eat something enchanting
High protein, slow-release carb foods are good for an afternoon energy boost. Prepare food the night before and do so with intention as this is what transforms an everyday snack into a magical pick-me-up. You could light a candle and speak a few words to bless your food and acknowledge its energy-giving qualities, for example.

Magical meditation
This meditation is a brilliant way to de-stress. Draw a tarot or oracle card and study the image as you take a few calming breaths, then imagine the image growing in size to become a frame that you can step through. Enter the image and look around. If the card features a person or creature, what might they say to you? If it is a landscape, how do you feel about the place? This exercise will give your subconscious a chance to make itself heard and can give you some interesting insights.

BREAK OUT YOUR BESOM

Witches' brooms are not just for transport: make your own mini-besom (broomsticks, usually made from birch) and use it to whisk away any negative energies during your break, so that you can start afresh in the afternoon.

MATERIALS:
FOR YOUR BESOM:
A twig
Scissors
Sandpaper
Dried grass, straw or rosemary stalks (for the bristles)
Twine

TO DECORATE IT:
Small feathers, ribbons, etc. (optional)

ALSO:
Cleaning spray and cloth
Enchanted room spray (see page 84)

To make your besom

Witches often use besoms to cleanse an area, and you can make a mini one very easily. Trim and sand down your twig to make it smooth. Gather your bristle material in small bunches and cut to an appropriate length for your broom. Tie each small bunch together, then arrange them around the end of your twig and fix securely to your 'broomstick'. You can add a decorative ribbon, rune or feathers to your ceremonial besom once finished if you like.

Get sweeping

Start by giving your work area a quick tidy and wipe down. Once it's physically clean you're ready to clear away any negative energy. Take your besom and whisk it around in an anticlockwise motion. You could visualize pure white light coming from the broom as you clear away any negative vibes. Give the air a spritz with your enchanted room spray (see page 84) if you like and then whisk your broom around in a clockwise direction, inviting in new and fresh energy for the afternoon ahead.

NOTE: If you don't have the materials to make a wooden besom, you can make a paper one from stationery supplies: a rolled-up tube of paper will do for the handle, and a Post-it note with 'bristles' cut up to the sticky tab can be rolled round it to form the end.

CHOC-ORANGE POSITIVITY BALLS

These indulgent snacks will boost your energy and your mood, too. You can mix in a little magic as you make them, along with the power of some witchy ingredients: orange promotes positivity, and cinnamon brings speedy results and success.

INGREDIENTS:
100 g (3 1/2 oz/1/2 cup) pitted dates (e.g. Medjool)
50 g (1 3/4 oz/1/4 cup) cashew nuts
50 g (1 3/4 oz/1/4 cup) walnuts
50 g (1 3/4 oz/1/4 cup) oats
3 tablespoons cacao powder
2 tablespoons almond or peanut butter
3 tablespoons orange juice
A pinch of cinnamon

Before you start your prep, you might like to add some magical touches to your worktop. You could light a candle, cast a circle and state your intention: to infuse your food with positivity and energy, for example.

Hold the ingredients in turn to charge them up before adding them to the food processor. Visualize warm, yellow-orange energy flowing from your heart, down your arms and into each ingredient. Pop everything into the mixer except the cinnamon, then whizz until the nuts are chopped and the mixture starts to come together. You can always add more orange juice if you prefer a softer consistency.

Finally, sprinkle in the cinnamon and stir it round, saying, 'With cinnamon I charge this spell, with gratitude I mix it.' Roll the mixture into balls of whatever size you like but bear in mind one large ball is not a good plan! For extra witchiness, you could carve a pentagram (to symbolize balance and protection) into each ball with the tip of a sharp knife.

Take your finished snack to work for a magical energy boost whenever you need one.

NOTE: You can experiment with different combinations of nuts and spices. The energy balls will keep for a couple of weeks in the fridge.

A 'POWER THROUGH YOUR TO-DO LIST' SPELL

It's lunchtime already and you've only ticked one thing off your to-do list. Even worse, that thing was 'have a coffee'. How can you pick up the pace and get productive in the afternoon?

So, what can you do about it?

Reach for your enchanted pen. It's a great tool to use at work in place of a wand. This spell is an example of how you can discreetly practise written witchery at your desk.

MATERIALS:
FOR YOUR PEN:
A posh pen (see below)
Salt, water, a candle and some incense

FOR THE SPELL:
Your enchanted pen
Paper
A shredder

To enchant your pen
Charge your pen up with magical energy at home on your altar. Set out a small bowl of salt to the north and water to the west, then some incense to the east and the candle to the south. Light the candle and the incense. Next sprinkle a little salt into the water and use a tissue to dab some of this along the pen, saying, 'With the power of earth and water I consecrate this pen for magic.' Take the pen and whisk it through the incense smoke and above the candle flame, saying, 'With the power of air and fire I consecrate this pen for magic.' Leave your pen on your altar overnight, wrapped in a soft cloth, and it will be ready to use as your workplace wand.

To power through your to-do list
Use your pen to jot down the things you want to achieve in the next few hours. Fold the piece of paper in on itself and draw a symbol on the outside. You could either draw a large tick, write 'Get this done' or create a sigil for this (see page 42). Activate your spell by destroying the paper and discarding the pieces.

Other ways to use your enchanted pen
Draw sigils or symbols in the air whenever you need a witchy power-up. Cast a protective circle around you; easily done on a swivel chair! Hex an annoying co-worker. Just subtly point your pen at your nemesis, sending an appropriate mental message their way: 'Be silent, arsling,' should do the trick. Just don't say this out loud.

6

THERE'S NO (EVIL) 'I' IN TEAM

You can choose your friends, but you can't (usually) choose your colleagues, which is a shame because having tricky people around you at work can really put a downer on your day. Luckily this is an area where a little covert witchcraft can help, whether you want to create an atmosphere of warmth and happiness in the workplace, spread some goodwill ... or use a little light hexing to take a tricky coworker down a notch.

YOU GOT THIS

A CANDLE SPELL FOR TEAM HARMONY

You're part of a new team at work and there's the usual eclectic mix of personalities; a couple of can't-be-bothered's; a quirky-but-quiet; and someone trying far too hard to act as peacemaker (you). How can you get your team to work together without going zorbing together, or spending a muddy weekend failing to build a tent in a field?

So, what can you do about it?

A simple candle spell will smooth things over and help your team to gel.

MATERIALS:
Several pinches of lavender (for peace)
Several pinches of basil leaves (for harmony)
A candle to represent each person on your team
Lavender, sage or patchouli oil

Mix the lavender and basil in a bowl and use these to dress one of your candles to represent you and your peace-making powers. First, lightly coat the candle with your chosen essential oil, excluding the wick. Focus on your intention of bringing harmony to your team while you do this, then roll the candle in the herb mix. Set this candle up in the middle of your altar. Dressing candles adds potency to your spell.

Scatter a circle of lavender and basil around your central candle. Now choose a candle for each of your team members. You could use different coloured candles to fit their personalities or use any colour and inscribe each person's initial near the top, focusing on their characteristics as you do it. Set them up one by one inside your circle.

Light the central candle and say, 'May this spell bring peace and harmony to our team.' Take each person's candle in turn and light it from the central flame, saying as you do so, '[Name of person], bring peace and harmony to our team.' When all the candles are alight, say:

We [insert number] people, let us gel

So we can work together well,

Smooth out our problems, quarrels end,

Help our energy to blend

And let them burn down until the initials have melted, to activate your spell.

SPRAY IT FORWARD

An enchanted room spray is an excellent way to spread a little subtle magic at work. It's simple to make: just combine water with vodka (for its preservative qualities) in a ratio of 60:40 in a dark-coloured spray bottle. You could use moon water, rainwater or water that has been set out in the sun for a few hours. Focus on your intention as you add around twenty drops of your chosen combination of oils (see below), testing the scent as you go, as essential oils vary in strength.

To spread positivity, you could use juniper and orange blossom, and pop in a few chips of rose quartz (to promote positive relationships). Give the room a spritz before your next team meeting and sit back to admire the results.

- Bergamot for prosperity
- Cedar for self-control
- Citrus for energy or a mood-boost
- Clove for counteracting negativity
- Eucalyptus for purification
- Frankincense for balance and to alleviate stress
- Jasmine for love and relaxation
- Juniper for protection and positivity
- Lavender for peace, calm and protection
- Lilac for harmony
- Magnolia for harmony and peace
- Myrrh for grounding and acceptance
- Neroli for joy and happiness
- Orange blossom for harmony and positivity
- Patchouli for love and lust. Just be careful where you spray this one!
- Peppermint for purification
- Pine for purification and cleansing
- Rose for tranquillity
- Saffron for calm
- Sandalwood for cleansing and protection
- Tea tree for cleansing and healing
- Vetiver for new beginnings
- Ylang-ylang for joy and enthusiasm

ELEMENTARY TEAMWORK

When you're working with a bunch of different personalities at work, there's sure to be the odd clash, but a little elementary witchcraft can help to keep things calm and balanced. The first step is working out your colleagues' personality types. Everyone has aspects of all four elements in their make-up, but often one will be dominant.

Earth people
Tend to be reliable, practical, grounded and down to earth

STRENGTHS: hard-working, organized
WEAKNESSES: can be judgemental and inflexible

Fire people
Tend to be charismatic, passionate, open

STRENGTHS: creative and enthusiastic
WEAKNESSES: can be impulsive and over-bearing

Air people
Tend to be logical, intelligent, curious

STRENGTHS: witty, independent, excellent problem-solvers
WEAKNESSES: can be inconsistent and cold

Water people
Tend to be empathetic, compassionate, trusting

STRENGTHS: caring and creative, good listeners
WEAKNESSES: can be over-sensitive and irrational

Once you've worked out your co-workers' characteristics, you can use this to your advantage. If you're putting together a team you could balance out a Fire person's enthusiasm by having them work with a grounded and practical Earth character. Or if you need a tricky one-to-one with an emotional Watery soul, you could prepare some calm and logical Air-type arguments to keep things on track.

You can also use elemental witchcraft if someone's characteristics are causing trouble at work.* For example:

To energize Earth: take a small stone to represent your problem person and carefully circle this a safe distance above a candle flame, saying, '[Name of person], I set you free, find Fire and creativity.'

To humanize Air: light an incense stick and focus on your co-worker, before dipping the end into water, saying, '[Name of person], fickle and cool, let your emotions flow and rule.'

To tame Fire: light a candle to represent your colleague and stand this in a small dish of earth, saying, '[Name of person]'s Fire burns too bright, I ground you to reduce your light.'

To anchor Water: place a small dish of water somewhere warm and leave this to evaporate, saying, '[Name of person], when your emotions overflow, cool them with Air, let logic show.'

If your working day involves lots of meetings with unfamiliar customers or clients, you can still use your witchy intuition to help you. Tune in to their energy level and adjust yours to match. If someone is upbeat and cheery, greeting them differently to someone who is quiet and reserved could make for a more positive interaction.

*NOTE: Casting a spell on someone without their consent is a form of hexing.

QUICK-FIX POSITIVITY TRICKS

If you want to banish negative vibes and encourage a feeling of harmony at work, you can use a little undercover witching to help. Items can easily be enchanted at home and set up in the office to spread some peace and happiness.

Secret shrine
Create a shrine to positivity in a communal area: you could include a peaceful picture or photograph in a frame, a dish containing moonstones (for harmony), with one to represent each team member, or a pot plant, such as lavender (for peace) or lemon balm (for healing).

Rose quartz
A great tool for promoting healing and love, rose quartz is easy enough to power up at home and bring into work. You can also buy ornaments made from rose quartz, to further disguise your magic. Enchant your stone(s) by setting them on an altar at home, lighting a candle (perhaps inscribed with a heart) and reciting a few words of peace and positivity as it burns.

Peace pot pourri
A bowl of pot pourri looks innocent enough but enchant it at home and you can add in harmonious vibes. To mix your own, combine dried petals (try rose and jasmine) with lavender and sage. As always, hold your intention in mind as you mix everything together. Add in a few drops of essential oil (see page 84); floral scents are a good choice as they promote harmony. Once that's done you have your peace in a pot!

A WORK-RELATIONSHIP READING

If you've got beef with a co-worker (or they've got beef with you), a tarot reading can help you get to the bottom of what's going on. You don't need to be an expert at reading the cards to do this. Just use your intuition, and the guidebook to your pack, to help you interpret the cards in this reading.

MATERIALS:
A candle, incense or meditative music to help you focus
A pack of tarot cards
Your journal and a pen

Set yourself up somewhere quiet to carry out your reading. Relax, ground yourself and think about the person in question before you draw your cards. You could say aloud: 'Help me explore my relationship with XX and move on in positivity.' Then deal the cards as shown below:

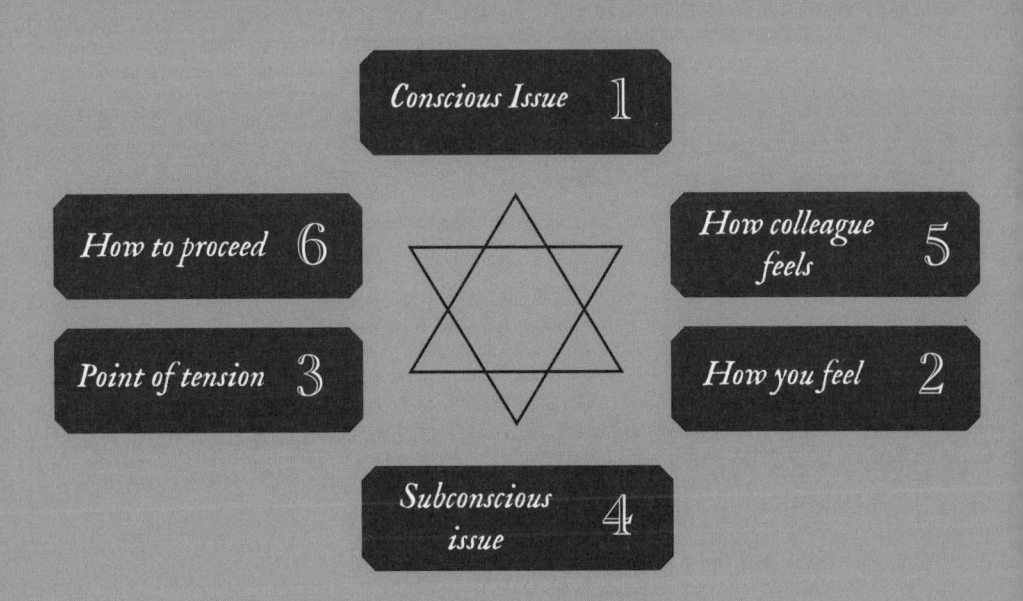

- Conscious Issue — 1
- How to proceed — 6
- Point of tension — 3
- Subconscious issue — 4
- How you feel — 2
- How colleague feels — 5

Consider each card in turn, studying the image and thinking about how it relates to your situation, before you turn to the guidebook. Afterwards, journal about what you've discovered and consider how you can move forward to a more positive footing.

BRIGHT BLESSINGS BISCUITS

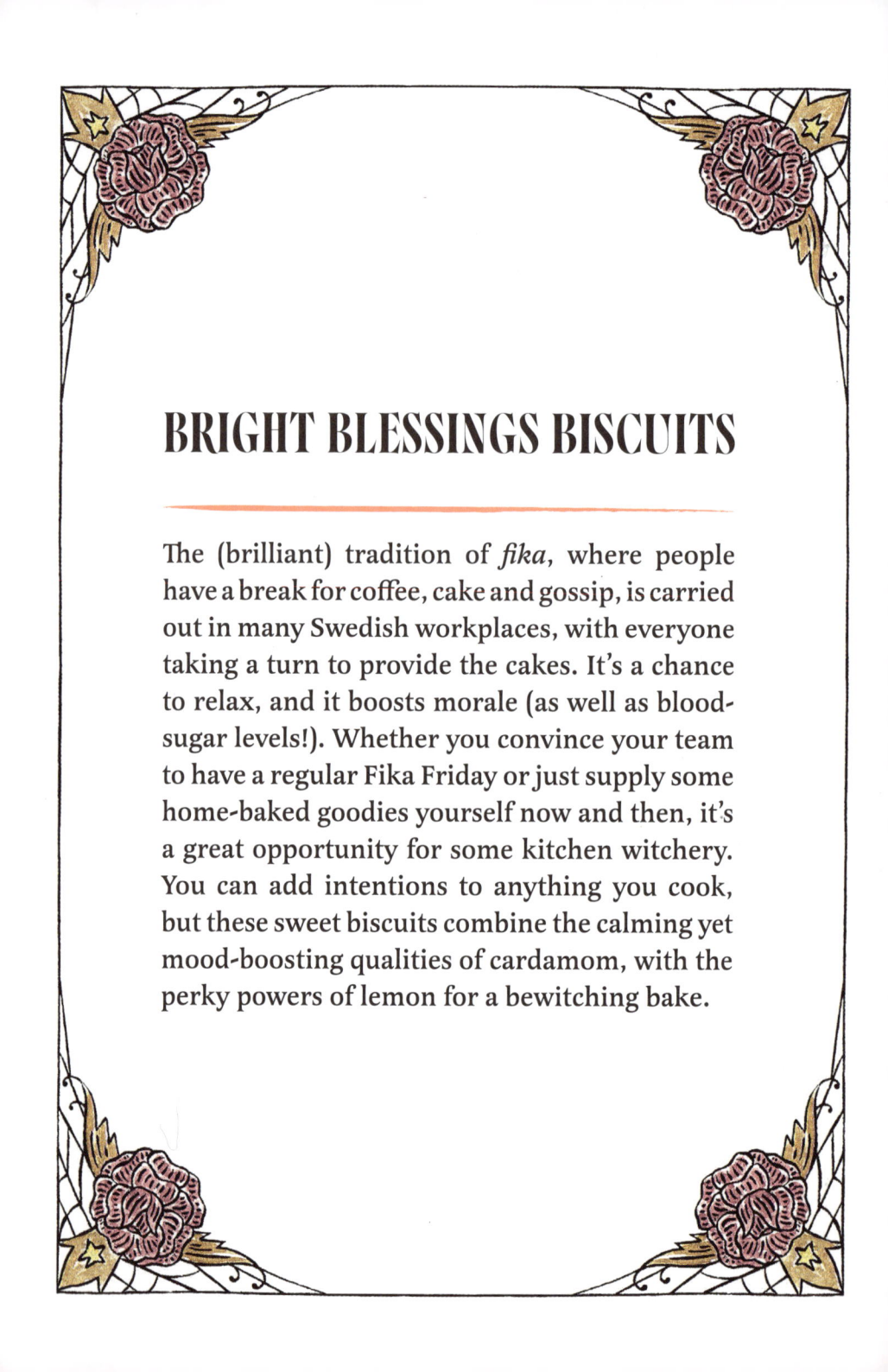

The (brilliant) tradition of *fika*, where people have a break for coffee, cake and gossip, is carried out in many Swedish workplaces, with everyone taking a turn to provide the cakes. It's a chance to relax, and it boosts morale (as well as blood-sugar levels!). Whether you convince your team to have a regular Fika Friday or just supply some home-baked goodies yourself now and then, it's a great opportunity for some kitchen witchery. You can add intentions to anything you cook, but these sweet biscuits combine the calming yet mood-boosting qualities of cardamom, with the perky powers of lemon for a bewitching bake.

MAKES AROUND 24 COOKIES

INGREDIENTS:
250g (9 oz/1 1/4 cups) plain flour
2 teaspoons ground cardamom
1 1/2 teaspoons baking powder
Zest of 4 lemons
225g (8 oz/ 1 cup) caster sugar
125g (4 oz/1/2 cup) butter, at room temperature
1 1/2 teaspoons vanilla extract
2 eggs
100g (3 1/2 oz/1/3 cup) icing sugar (for dusting)

Preheat the oven to 190°C (375°F). Combine all the dry ingredients in a bowl: the flour, cardamom, baking powder and lemon zest. As you add each ingredient, remember to focus on your intention to bring happiness and goodwill to your workmates.

In a separate bowl, beat the sugar into the butter until light and fluffy, then add in the vanilla extract and the eggs, one at a time, beating to combine. Stir in the dry ingredients in a clockwise direction, adding a healthy portion of positivity and happiness as you go.

Use your hands to gather the dough into a large ball and let this chill in the fridge for half an hour or so. Remove the dough and form it into 3 1/2 cm (1 1/4 inch) balls, rolling each in the icing sugar before flattening onto lined baking trays. Allow some room for them to spread out. Cook for 12 to 14 minutes, until they turn golden brown.

7

SHOW ME THE MONEY

Your job should challenge you and give you a sense of purpose, but most importantly it should be a source of cold, hard cash ... hopefully enough to pay the bills, buy some treats and stash some away as savings, too. If your salary isn't up to scratch, a little witchery can ensure that your skills and hard work are properly rewarded. The most successful money spells are not those where you request a million-pound lottery win, but if you ask the Universe to provide what you need while taking some practical steps in the right direction yourself, you'll be pleasantly surprised at the results.

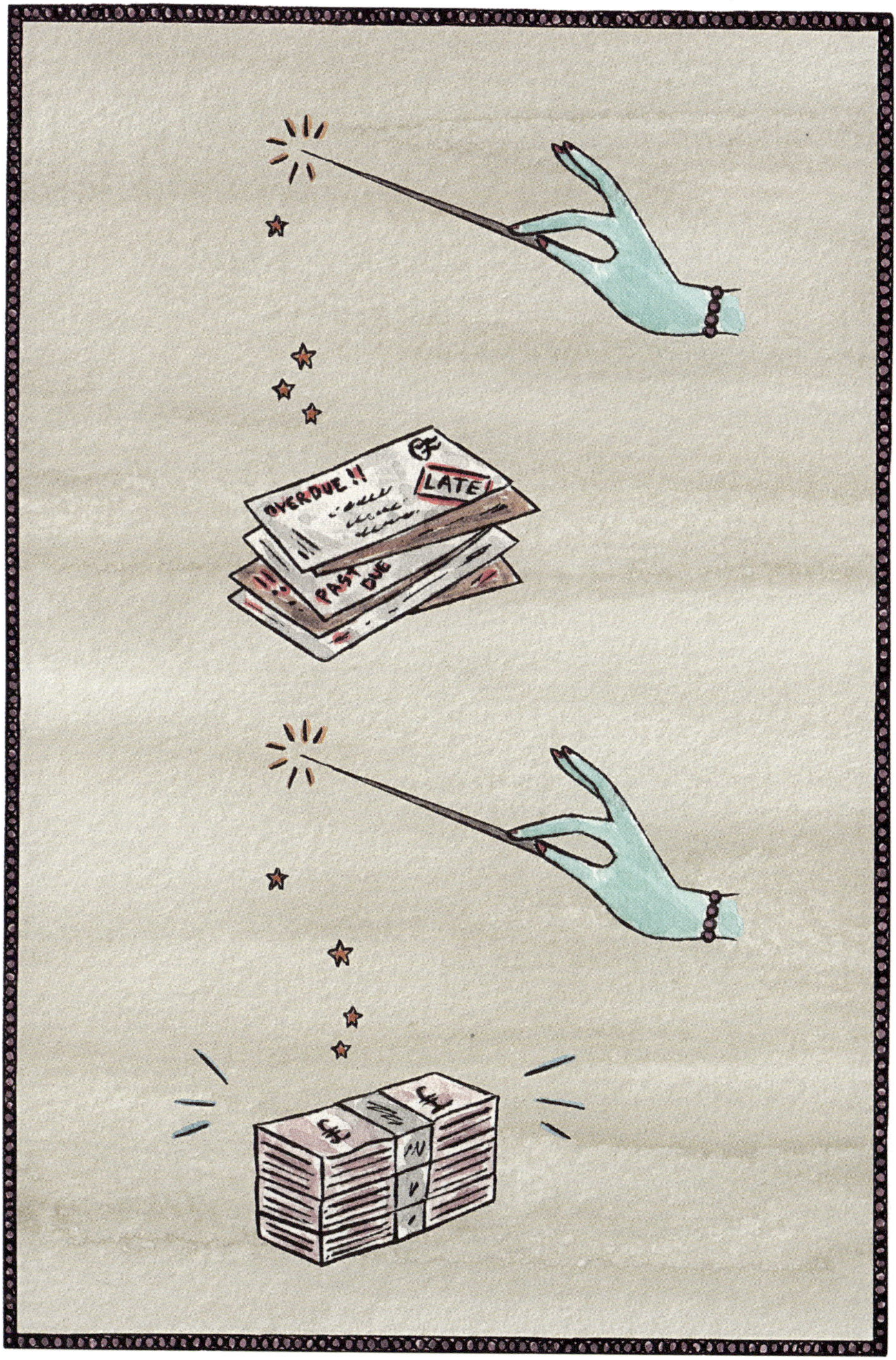
OVERDUE !!
LATE
PAST DUE

A SUITABLE SALARY SPELL

You've got a final interview for a new job; you're sure to get it, but you want to be prepared to negotiate your starting salary: there's a 5k range on the ad, so how can you get top whack?

So, what can you do about it?

You need to be ready to negotiate, and for that, research is key. This ritual is a nice one to carry out as you do a bit of pre-negotiation prep. Set up your cauldron, filled with prosperity-boosting witchy items, and combine magic with research to get the perfect salary.

MATERIALS:
A small cauldron or bowl
Several handfuls of dried rice
A tealight
A piece of aventurine crystal
Money-drawing oil, optional (see page 102)
Some bay leaves
A flameproof saucer

Add a good layer of rice to your cauldron and place the tealight in the centre. Put the aventurine crystal alongside it and add a few drops of money-drawing oil to the cauldron if you have it. Light the tealight, then do the research.

Compare your job's salary range with similar roles advertised online to get a good idea of a fair wage. Consider your skills and experience, making a note of these in case you need to back up your request, and decide on the minimum salary that would be acceptable to you. Make sure you factor in any travel expenses or other costs you might have.

Write your goal salary down on one of the bay leaves. Now add around 15 per cent to that figure and write it on the other side. This will be your starting point in case you need to negotiate. If there are other benefits you would like as part of the deal, such as a gym membership or a company car, for example, write these on other leaves, too. You can use slips of paper instead, if using all the bay leaves means you will have nothing left to cook with.

Set fire to the leaves from the tealight, saying, 'In return for my skills, I ask for this reward,' for each one. Drop the burning leaves onto a flameproof saucer, then take the ashes outside and blow or scatter them to activate your spell.

AN ABUNDANCE ALTAR

It's easy to make an altar to invite abundance and wealth into your life. You can dedicate a small space to this at home, and use it to carry out prosperity spells, or set up a shrine at work. Feng shui tells us a corner is best, so that all that lovely prosperous energy can accumulate in the space. Here are some ideas of what you could include.

Green candles

A small pot or dish containing rice or coins. Try including different currencies if you want to travel. Add and remove coins every now and then to invite financial exchange.

Bay leaves (with or without witchy symbols on them)

A four-leaf clover symbol or image

Pentacle symbols, charms or tarot cards

Jade or citrine crystals

A money plant or jade plant

Cinnamon or sandalwood incense

Prosperity oil (see page 102)

Cinnamon sticks

A statuette of your chosen deity or a Chinese lucky cat

NOTE: Think about why you want to attract more money into your life. Do you want to buy a home, go travelling, or save up for something specific? Include an item that represents this intention on your altar, too.

A SIMMER POT OF PROSPERITY

Here's a spell to fill your surroundings with the scent of some top-notch kitchen witchery. It's perfect if you work from home or have access to a cooktop at work, where it will encourage your customers to linger and spend a lot more cash.

MATERIALS:
A large heat-proof cauldron or pan
Water
1 bay leaf
1 lemon, sliced
1 orange, cut into rough quarters
3 cinnamon sticks
1 star anise
1 tablespoon ground nutmeg

Gather your items and give your hob-top a physical and magical cleanse with moon water (see page 45) before you start witching.

Pour fresh water into your cauldron and set it to simmer. Take the bay leaf and spend a moment thinking about what prosperity means and feels like to you, then draw a pound or dollar sign on the leaf. Swirl it into the water.

Add the other ingredients one at a time, pausing as you hold each and revisiting that feeling of prosperity.

Let the pot simmer away and fill your room with its magical aroma. Do check your potion now and then to see if it needs a top-up. When you're ready to dispose of your simmer pot components, drain away any remaining water and compost the rest ... apart from the pan!

'PAY RISE, PLEASE!' MONEY-DRAWING OIL

The day has come: it's time for your work-based wonderfulness to be properly rewarded, so you're going to ask for a pay rise. But what can you do before you sit down with your boss to ensure they don't say, 'Sorry, we haven't got the budget'?

So, what can you do about it?

Before you get witching, be sure to prepare for your meeting and make a case for why you deserve the extra dosh. Make a list of everything you've done over the past few months to benefit the business. Do some research into the average wage for your role to ensure your pay packet measures up. Then, head to the kitchen and mix yourself some money-drawing oil before you sit down to negotiate that raise.

MATERIALS:
A green candle
A toothpick or pin
A small, clean bottle
1 teaspoon cloves
1 teaspoon basil
1 teaspoon mint
1 bay leaf
1 cinnamon stick, broken into pieces
Olive oil

Inscribe the rune for wealth, Fehu (see page 131), towards the top of your candle using a toothpick. Light the candle and circle the flame with the bottle at a safe distance above the flame, saying:

This oil I mix to conjure wealth

Bless this spell to bring myself

The pay I'm owed, the funds I'm due,

Make my wages fair and true

Add the dry components to the bottle first, keeping your intention for a positive pay-rise result in mind as you do it. Then add olive oil to fill the bottle and pop in the cork. Hold it in your hands and visualize abundant bright golden light spreading out from the bottle. Keep the bottle next to the candle until the Fehu rune has been burned away.

Let the oil steep for 24 hours, or from the new to full moon if you're super-organized and have planned ahead.

Apply a few dots of the oil to your wrists before you take the plunge and ask for your pay boost. You can also add a discreet dot to any paperwork you take into the meeting. Keep the rest to use in other spellwork such as anointing candles, for example.

SHOW ME THE MONEY

QUICK-FIX MONEY TRICKS

There are plenty of speedy spells you can do to conjure up some extra money, whether it's a bonus in your next pay packet, a small but handy lotto win or a surprise paid side hustle.

Lucky penny
Charge up a lucky penny on your money altar: you could carry out a ritual with a green candle anointed with money-drawing oil (see page 102) and speak your intention for the coin to bring you extra funds. Then carry the penny in your purse or keep it in the till at work, if you run your own business, to attract extra wealth. You can also do this with an aventurine crystal, the stone most often used in abundance spells.

Plant a seed
If you're starting a new business venture or project, plant a seed at the next new moon and speak a few words to link the plant's progress with your plans: 'As this plant thrives, so my business grows,' for example. Tend to your plant carefully and spend a moment beside it every day, visualizing a successful venture.

Bay-leaf bonanza
When you're spellcasting for money, reach for the bay leaves; they are often used to attract wealth. Be specific and design a sigil (see page 42) that sums up why you need the funds, then carry the bay leaf in your purse or include it in one of the other spells in this chapter.

Pay it forward
Light a candle and meditate for a while on what abundance means to you. Think about why you want to attract more money, what you would use it for and how this would bring you happiness. When you do receive a bonus, it's a nice idea to give a little back to the Universe in thanks by giving a small donation to a charity. Even a coin in a collection bucket sends out the message that you're grateful for what the 'verse has gifted you.

SIX PENTACLES TO BAG A BARGAIN

Money spells aren't just about raking in financial rewards; they can help save on your outgoings, too. If you run a small business and need to purchase stock or equipment, like that fancy coffee machine for the staffroom, getting a good price will keep your accountant happy come the end of the year. Of course, this spell can be used to negotiate a good deal for non-work-related spends, too.

MATERIALS:
The Six of Pentacles tarot card (optional)
Six tokens or coins (all of the same type)
Your wand or enchanted pen (see page 78)

This spell tunes in to the energy of the Six of Pentacles, which is the card associated with fair prices and honest dealing. Before you make your purchase, study the card, or a just a picture of it, and meditate on the image. What do you think would be a fair offer for the goods you're going to buy?

Next, set out the six coins or tokens, either side of your laptop or phone, in two neat stacks of three. If you're negotiating via email, compose your message; if you'll be making an offer over the phone, key in the phone number, but don't press 'call' just yet. First take your wand (or pen) and draw six pentacles in the air above the screen, saying:

*I've made my cash and
guard it well,*

So save me money with this spell,

Six pentacles here: three and three

To fix the fairest price for me

Then send your message, or make the call, and let the Universe do the rest.

8

WHEREVER I LAY MY BROOM ...

If you're less office-based and more 'all over the place', working and witching can be a little more challenging. Perhaps you move from company to company or client to client and find yourself heading off to your next placement before you've even had a chance to hang up your cloak. Well, never fear, there's always a way to cast a little magic, whether you're working from a hotel room, a hot desk or your car.

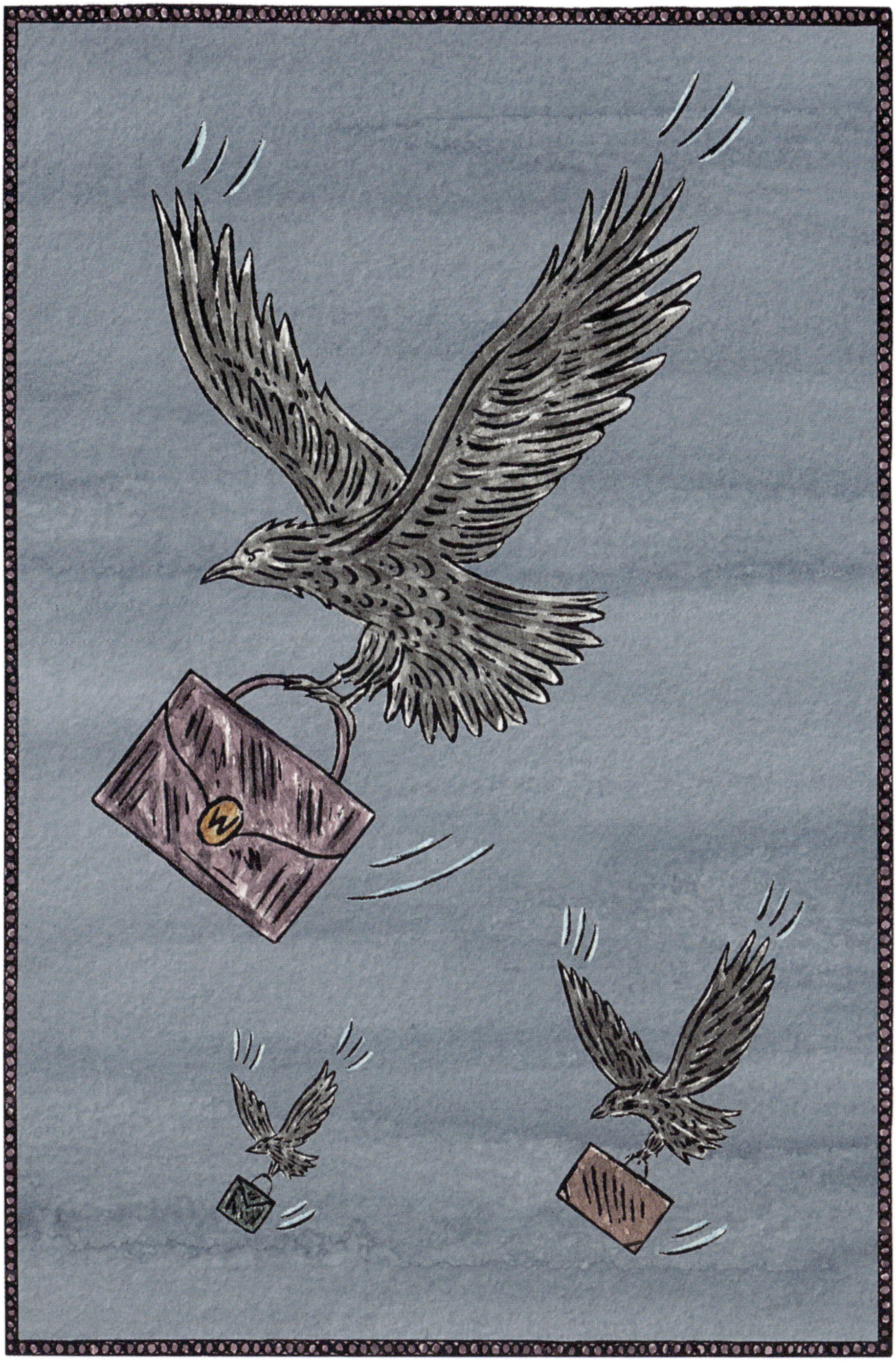

CHARGING UP A GROUNDING STONE

This simple visualization will help you feel grounded wherever your working day takes you. Choose a solid stone that feels weighty in your hands rather than a tumblestone (a small, polished crystal). You could use a pebble, or a larger crystal, but jasper and tourmaline are good for grounding, too. I have a piece of haematite that fits exactly in my palm.

MATERIALS:
Your grounding stone
A calming piece of music
To charge the stone:
Your favourite incense

First enhance your stone's connection with the earth by cleansing it with incense or running water, then burying it in the ground for a night or two. Resurrect your stone and clean it, ready to charge it up.

Light the incense and play your music; something instrumental will work well as you won't be distracted by lyrics. Sit on the floor holding the stone in your palm and relax into the moment. Focus on the weight of the stone and the way it's pulling down towards the earth.

Take some deep, calming breaths, and visualize a ball of copper-coloured energy swirling inside the stone and then flowing through you down towards the earth. The energy feels comforting, heavy and warm as it moves through you and anything separating you from the ground. It continues through the soil, past the roots of plants and animals' burrows. It passes rocks and boulders, on and on until it reaches the mantle beneath the planet's crust, and then ever downwards to the planet's core.

Feel the weight of the connection anchoring you to Earth. When you're ready, imagine the energy trail gently disconnecting from the core and threading all the way back to the stone in your hand.

Take your grounding stone with you on your work travels and use it every day to reconnect to this calming and comforting energy, by repeating the visualization with your chosen music on.

AN ANTI-STRESS AMULET RITUAL

If your work involves responding to emergencies or people in distress, it can be hard to find time for so much as a bathroom break, let alone proper self-care. This amulet can be charged up and used to help you gather and protect yourself before or after attending a difficult incident.

MATERIALS:
Your choice of token for your amulet
A black candle

You can use any small item to be the base of your amulet. This could be a coin, gem or a figurine, or even a collection of small objects in a pouch. Enchant your amulet by casting a circle and setting the item(s) inside it next to the candle. Inscribe a protection rune such as Algiz (see page 143), for example, on your amulet and on the candle. As the candle burns down past the rune, visualize a bubble of pale blue protective energy spreading out from the amulet, as you recite:

This amulet shields me from harm,

It keeps me safe; it keeps me calm

Let the shield expand to enclose you and breathe into the feeling of being protected and secure. Extinguish the candle and close the circle. Your amulet is now charged.

Repeat the visualization during your working day when you need to invoke a feeling of safety or calm. Hold the amulet and let the bubble spread out, surround and shield you, reminding you that you're not a part of the cause or effect of the incident or situation. You could combine this with tapping to release stress: a quick ritual could include holding the amulet while focusing on your breathing and tapping your collarbones.

Using the amulet can be an effective way of dealing with the short-term stress of your role, but don't forget to make use of all the support available to you to look after your mental health. Also, thank you for working in a difficult role – you're wonderful.

QUICK-FIX CAR-BASED TRICKS

When your working day consists of driving from one appointment to the next, it's a good plan to keep some magical items in your car to help you access your Boss Witch powers whatever the day brings.

MATERIALS:
A protective amulet (see page 126)
A come-home stone (see page 55)
A portable altar (in a container that fits in the glove box, or under one of the seats)
A set of tarot or oracle cards
A safe-travel pouch (see page 55)
Some witchy snacks
A grounding stone (see page 110)

A parking-space spell

The tricky thing about parking-space magic is that you've got your hands on the steering wheel when you're searching for a space, so you can't really break out your wand. The best plan is to say your request out loud. It's a shame there's no parking deity to invoke. The gods were around 50,000 years too early for us to have a specific parking god, which is also why we don't have a printer god or a connecting-to-the-WiFi-on-public-transport god, sadly.

You could reach out to Hermes, Greek god of journeys (among other things), or Abeona, the Roman goddess of safe outward travels, who with her partner Adiona, the goddess of safe return, will have your whole journey covered. You could carry a symbol of one of these deities in your car, and ask for their help when needed, or simply ask the Universe to help you in your quest.

ALTARS ON THE GO

A mobile altar is the perfect solution if you travel a lot. You can either create one on your laptop or phone or keep some magical supplies in a small box to take with you when you're staying away; there's only so much improvising you can do with a trouser press, a mini-soap and a teabag.

TECH ALTARS

Having an altar as your desktop means you can tune in to your witchiness at the start of every work session (witch's hat optional). You can use a photo of your altar at home, a pic sourced online or an AI-generated altar (just specify the items you'd like to include), or create a collage of images that represent the elements, candles, gems and any deities you would include on an altar IRL.

AN ALTAR IN A BOX

You could include:

A scarf to use as an altar cloth

A small dish (to hold Water)

A feather (to represent Air)

A stone or crystal (to represent Earth)

A battery-operated tealight (to represent Fire)

A twig for a wand

Any other small natural items

A miniature bottle of essential oil

A miniature bottle of mixed herbs that you've charged up or blessed at home for general spellwork

A small, ornate box in which to keep everything

A 'LEAVE ME BE' SPELL WHEN WORKING FROM HOME

You're working from home and you're determined to have a super-productive day, but you've had phone calls from your relatives, parcels to take in for your neighbours and your cat keeps asking to be fed every five minutes. How can you do some work without any more disruptions?

So, what can you do about it?

A simple 'do not disturb' spell is the answer. You can cast this with your phone, with a wand, or go old school and scatter protection powder on the floor. The plus-side of working from home is that it's your floor, so you can scatter whatever the heck you like on it.

MATERIALS:
Your phone or your wand or a bowl of 'protection powder' (see below)

Phone method
Use your phone camera to cast a circle around your work area by taking a panoramic shot. Start in the north and slowly turn clockwise, visualizing a barrier around you as you create the photo. The picture doesn't need to be perfect, just make sure that you stop at the same point you started. As you turn, recite:

My circle's cast to set this space
For peaceful working in this place,
No interruptions shall I see
So may all others leave me be

Keep the photo until you finish work, then close your circle by taking a picture in the opposite direction, imagining your barrier dissolving, and then delete both pictures.

Wand method
Use your wand to cast a circle as you visualize your do-not-disturb boundary, reciting the same incantation as you do so.

Protection powder
Finely crush some eggshell (used as a symbol of protection) and mix this with some salt and sage in a bowl, focusing on your intention for some privacy as you do so. Cast a circle by scattering this around your work area repeating the incantation above. (Do not use this method if you have pets that might lick the powder; especially that hungry cat!) Clear away the circle by sweeping anticlockwise when your work is done.

SAFE HEXING

If you haven't worked with hexes before you may be wondering what's involved. Are you taking a step into the dark side and will you be cursed if you give them a try? Well, the hexes in this book are designed to be used in self-defence, to empower you to stand up for yourself and heal after being treated badly. As long as your spell is justified, the Universe won't punish you for this. Even if you believe in the Threefold Law, which states anything you deal out will be served back to you but three times stronger, remember that what you are dealing out here is an act of self-care, rather than bad vibes and evil intentions.

It is important to think carefully before carrying out a hex, though. Casting a spell that affects another person is a big step and takes a lot of energy, too. Is it the right thing to do? A good rule is to never hex in anger; make sure everything is calm, considered and grounded. Whatever your potential hexee's offence against you, think about their motivation. If your hot-desk buddy left your workstation in a mess again, they were probably in a rush, rather than setting out to spoil your morning, so having a chat with them rather than hexing them is the right way to go. But if you're being bullied or badly treated and you have no other way to set things right, using a hex is absolutely justified.

When hexing, be sure to cast a protective circle (see page 124), to cleanse everything thoroughly before and after your spell, and to leave a window open if you're evicting bad energy as it needs somewhere to go.

9

GHOSTS IN THE BOARDROOM

It's never the good stuff we remember, is it? If you get one hundred positive customer reviews and one negative one, there are no prizes for guessing which you'll dwell on. Hanging on to the past, especially the negative stuff, only stops you enjoying and achieving in the present, so use a little hexing to exorcise those ghosts. Hexing is a magical form of self-defence, which can involve healing, binding and banishing, as well as baneful spells. And as always, when things get hexy, it's important to use some protection.

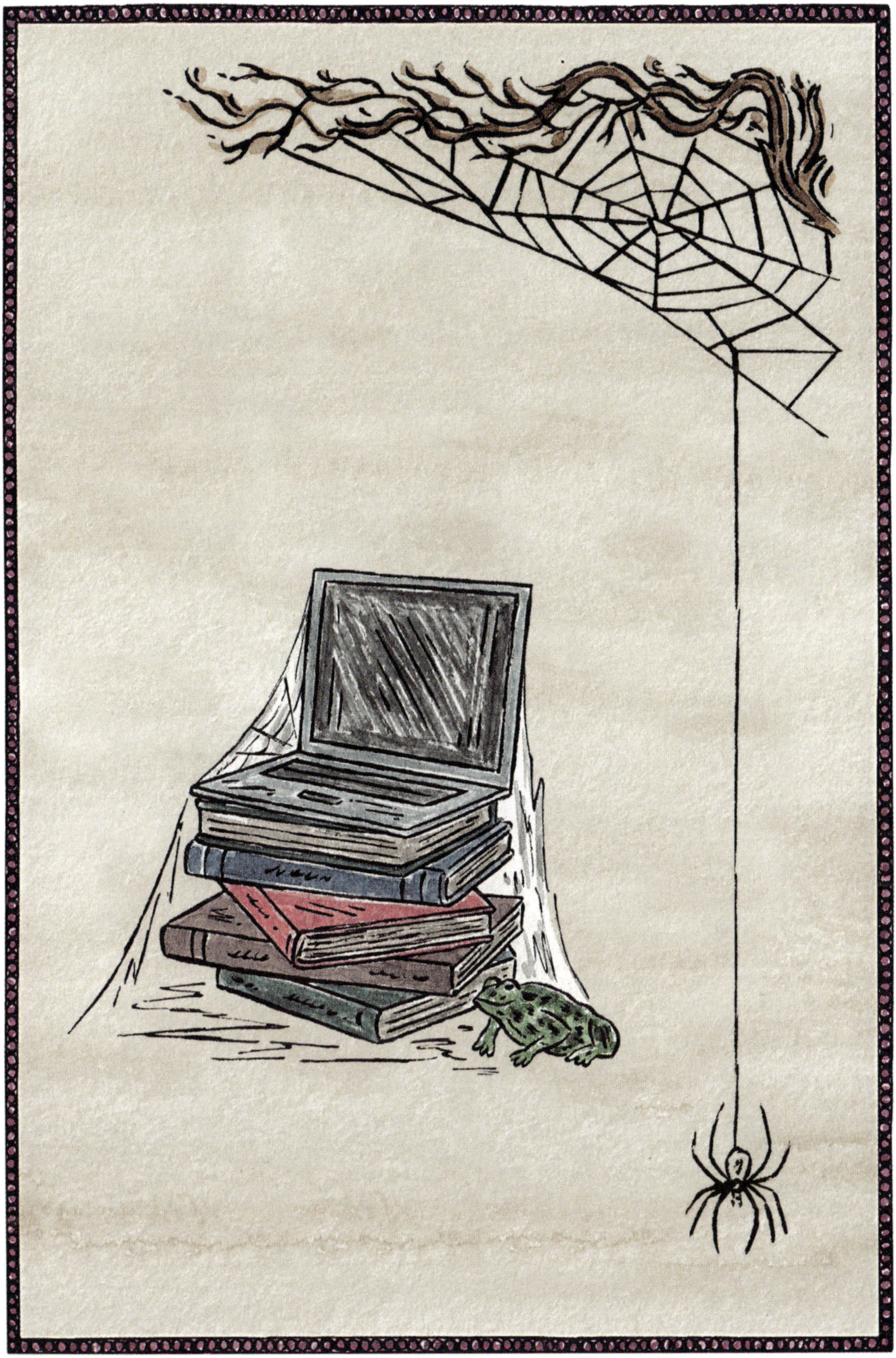

QUICK-FIX PROTECTION TRICKS

It's good practice to cast a protective circle whenever you wave your wand, but when you're working with negative energies, you should step up the protection. Here are some ideas, which you can combine or use individually.

MATERIALS:
Use cedar incense or a smudge stick to mark a protective circle around you. Sprinkle protection powder (see page 119) around you to create a safe boundary.

Cast a circle using your wand for added power. At the north call in the guardians of the Earth element, that is the Page, Knight, Queen and King of Pentacles from the tarot, to stand before you, facing outwards. At the east invite in the guardians of Air, namely the Swords court cards, in a similar way. Do the same for the south (Fire/Wands) and the west (Water/Cups). You could arrange the tarot cards for these 16 powerful guardians around you as you picture them standing in a protective ring, keeping you safe. After your spell, thank them and allow them to leave.

Visualize a solid, protective shield around you: after grounding yourself, picture the aura of energy that cocoons you as a cloud of shifting colours. Now see the outer edges of this cloud becoming solid to form your shield. This may appear like a clear layer of ice, it may be metallic or wooden ... whatever substance feels safe and impenetrable to you. You can allow this barrier to soften and disperse when your hex is over.

I also have a symbolic protective ring on my altar. Mine consists of a circle of six carved wooden figures that I was gifted, seated around a wooden 'fire'. I have a small pewter figure, which represents me, sitting safely inside this circle of wisdom and magic. You could create one using crystals, shells, a necklace ... anything that is symbolic or relevant to you.

MAKING AN EVIL-EYE AMULET

The protective power of the evil eye has been used for at least 3,000 years across many cultures. The eye sees off the malicious gaze of anyone wishing you harm, so be sure to wear one the next time you face up to your work nemesis across a meeting table. This amulet combines the power of this ancient symbol with the protective energies of your ancestors for you, their offspring!

MATERIALS:
A photograph of a parent, grandparent or relative (optional)
A lock of your hair
White, air-dry polymer clay
A skewer
Acrylic paints in dark blue, black and white and a brush
Air-dry clay glaze
A jewellery chain or cord

Gather your materials and cleanse them with sound or incense. Cast an extra protective circle around your working area (see page 124) and set up the photo of your loved-one in front of you.

Cut a small lock of your hair and visualize your parent(s) standing behind you with a hand on your shoulder, sending you positive vibes, love and protection. Now picture their parents behind them sending power through them into you. Continue to picture your ancestors further and further back and feel their strength, wisdom and love flowing into you. These guardians are represented in your DNA, in the lock of hair you hold.

Break off a piece of the clay, roll it into a ball and flatten it slightly. Now, place your lock of hair in the centre, fold the clay over to cover it, and shape into a flattened circle. As you do so, say:

May my ancestors protect me,

May their strength and love sustain me,

May this eye see off all evil,

May this pendant keep me safe

Use the skewer to pierce a hole at the top, to thread your cord or chain through. When the clay is dry, paint the pendant in the traditional evil-eye pattern, mixing the dark blue and white paint to form the pale blue colour. Add a layer of the glaze, once the paint is dry, and complete the amulet with the cord.

CORD-CUTTING AFTER AN OFFICE ROMANCE

So, you had a fling with a colleague, but now things have ended and there's some awkward energy buzzing around every time you bump into each other. How can you cut the connection between the two of you and get back to being co-workers rather than exes?

So, what can you do about it?

A classic cord-cutting spell is the answer, so get your candles out, unshackle yourself from the past and move forward without your office baggage dragging along behind you.

MATERIALS:
A black candle, for the person you need to banish
A candle of your choosing, to represent you
A toothpick or pin
A few drops each of sage and vetiver essential oils
A heatproof dish
A piece of hemp, string or twine
A slip of paper and a pen

Carve a symbol or initials onto the candles to symbolize yourself and your office ex. Concentrate on the connection you want to sever as you do this: the more intention you put in at this stage, the more powerful your ritual will be.

Anoint the black candle with the sage essential oil for banishing negativity and your candle with vetiver, for new beginnings. Melt the base of each candle and stand them a few centimetres apart in the heatproof dish. Tie the string in a loop around the two candles about two-thirds of the way up. Write on the slip of paper a word or two about what you want to release.

Light the candles and light your slip of paper from the black one. Drop this into the heatproof dish and say,

> *The bond we made is ending now*
>
> *I cut the tie, move on,*
>
> *My flame burns bright, unfettered*
>
> *Your influence is gone*

Sit with your candles and your thoughts. When the cord catches fire, visualize the link between you and your ex breaking. Wait for the candles to burn down and, once everything has cooled, dispose of the remains in the bin.

This can be a draining spell, so nurture yourself afterwards, and remember that if you were hurt during the fling or break-up, you may need time and support to fully heal.

IT'S A SIGN!

Symbols can be a potent part of spellcasting, focusing your intentions and helping you to manifest great results. Whatever charm you're working there's sure to be a symbol you can use to enhance it. Whether you display it on your desktop, draw it on your wrist or fashion it out of your paperclip stash, you can call on the ancient energy of these symbols to augment your magic.

The triple moon
Combining the three phases of the moon, this symbol can be used in spells involving transition: progressing from the start of a project to its fruition.

Pentacle
Representing full Boss Witch power, protection and balance, this symbol can be used to enhance any magic. It's good for grounding meditations and also represents wealth and money.

Air
Linked with clear and logical thinking, the element of Air is an excellent addition to spells involving decision-making.

Water
Water represents emotion and empathy, so this symbol can be used when you're building understanding and positive relationships with co-workers.

Fire
Do you need to add a little passion to a project, get fired up for a presentation or increase your motivation? The Fire element will give you a boost.

Earth
Great for grounding when you're stressed or need bringing back down to Earth, this symbol adds a calm, considered element to your magic.

Fehu
This ancient rune represents wealth, success and reward, making it excellent for any spell involving career progression.

Rebirth
Use this when you want to clear the decks and start afresh – with a new project or even a new career.

Money
Carry this in your purse; pop it on your altar or inscribe it on a green candle and burn to activate your desire for more funds.

The sun
The sun represents confidence, creativity and self-esteem, so incorporate it into your spellwork at the start of a new project, or when you need a boost in these areas.

The moon
The moon represents the importance of trusting your intuition, especially when deception or trickery are taking place. Use it in spells to help you get in touch with your inner wisdom and find a safe path forward.

Philosopher's stone
Representing knowledge and understanding, this is a useful symbol for conjuring success in a test or when putting together a speech or report.

Awen
This ancient Celtic symbol incorporates three rays of light and represents creativity and inspiration, making it perfect for spells involving new projects and ideas.

Water droplet
Use for purification spells, when clearing negative energy or bad memories.

'LOSING THE LABELS' MOON RITUAL

There are places where labels are useful, such as a cupboard full of tin cans, and places where they're not. Labelling ourselves and others can be limiting: we forget that we're complex individuals with more to offer than a label may suggest. Here's a ritual to help you give negative labels a roasting and break free of their restrictions.

MATERIALS:
Pens or pencils
Matches
Something to write on (it could be leaves, tissues, paper or anything else your imagination comes up with)

In the days leading up to the full moon, give some thought to the labels you would like to lose. Perhaps you have always been told you are disorganized and the label has stuck. Perhaps you define yourself as 'just' an admin assistant, forgetting how you excel at your job … and the amazing voluntary work you do with kids at the weekends. Decide on the label(s) you want to shed.

Every evening, from full moon to new moon, you're going to do something to exorcise these limiting identities. You could make this a ritual each time by casting a circle, lighting a black candle and then performing your 'exorcism'. Use your imagination, but here are some ideas for ditching those labels:

- Write them on paper and burn them
- Write them on a leaf and let it blow away in the wind
- Write them on a tissue and blow your nose on it!
- Write them on a stone and throw it into the sea
- Put them in an envelope, seal it and then shred it
- List them in a document then delete it
- Carve them into a piece of soap, then wash them away

You can also visualize many (amusing) ways of getting rid of your limiting labels: blast them into space or send them back in time to get trampled by a dinosaur or drained by a bloodsucking vampire!

On the night of the dark moon, celebrate shedding your limitations with any treat you choose, and embrace a new challenge or hobby as the moon waxes.

WITCHES GET PROMOTED

BOTTLE THE BAD VIBES

Everyone has the odd off day at work, but if you're having a run of bad luck, or feel that your day-to-day work is being over-shadowed by a slip-up or negative experience, it's time to leave the past behind and bury those bad memories... literally.

MATERIALS:
A small bottle with a lid
Rusty and bent nails or pins
Some salt
A red ribbon or thread
Some vinegar
A black candle

Witches' bottles have long been used to get rid of negative vibes and they're easy to make. First, cleanse the bottle, then half-fill it with rusty nails (or anything pointy – to puncture your bad memories). Add the salt for protection, and then the red ribbon to bind those negative vibes. State your intention for each item you add to the jar as you go.

Now you need to add liquid to complete the spell. Some witches use their urine to literally tell the bad memories to pee off. If you, understandably, don't fancy that, vinegar will work just as well. Finish by putting the stopper or lid on top, and seal it with melted wax from the black candle.

The final step is to bury the bottle outside, if possible, or in the bottom of a planter, reciting:

These memories I pierce and drown

Their power o'er me is gone,

I bury them beneath the ground

Happy to move on.

A RITUAL FOR MOVING ON FROM REJECTION

Whether it's a job application or your latest manuscript that's been turned down, it can be hard not to take rejection personally, and even harder to move on with a spring in your step, ready to apply for new opportunities. However, this ritual will help you do just that.

MATERIALS:
Your favourite incense or scented candle
A piece of paper and an ink pen
A bowl of water
Some chocolate and/or your favourite drink

Light the candle or incense. Sage is a good choice as it helps clear negative energy and helps you to move on. Sit for a moment with your thoughts and remind yourself that rejection is never personal. You are, no-doubt, brilliant at what you do, but there may be many reasons you're not aware of why you were turned down. Perhaps an internal candidate was a shoo-in for the job, and the decision was made before you applied. Perhaps the publisher you chose has a quota to fill and isn't looking to publish something in your genre right now.

Your application may still yield results. With your details on file, you may have set yourself up for future success.

Your task now is to apply for plenty of things, not to succeed every time. You've done exactly what's necessary to get one step closer to your goal.

Acknowledge the feeling of disappointment, and any constructive feedback you can take on board moving forward. Then, write the name of the job and/or person you applied to on the paper. Drop this in the water, saying:

The choice made by these people

Does not reflect on me,

I welcome fresh beginnings

And opportunities

Submerge the paper and watch the ink running, until the words are unreadable. Dispose of the paper and water and treat yourself to a celebratory chocolate or drink. Congratulate yourself on having the confidence to put yourself out there. You're one step closer to success.

10

PAYBACK'S A WITCH

What if your work colleague is more than just a pain in the backside? Maybe you're facing up to a full-on bully every day, or you're dealing with a gaslighter, or working with a team member whose bitter behaviour is causing you (and probably everyone else) distress. It's time to break out some more Boss Witch hexes to help you make a stand and end the upset. These spells are not about hurting your coworker, but they are about protecting and standing up for yourself. As you'll be dealing with negative energies, remember to cast some extra protection (see page 124) when you use them and check out the warnings on page 120 about hexing.

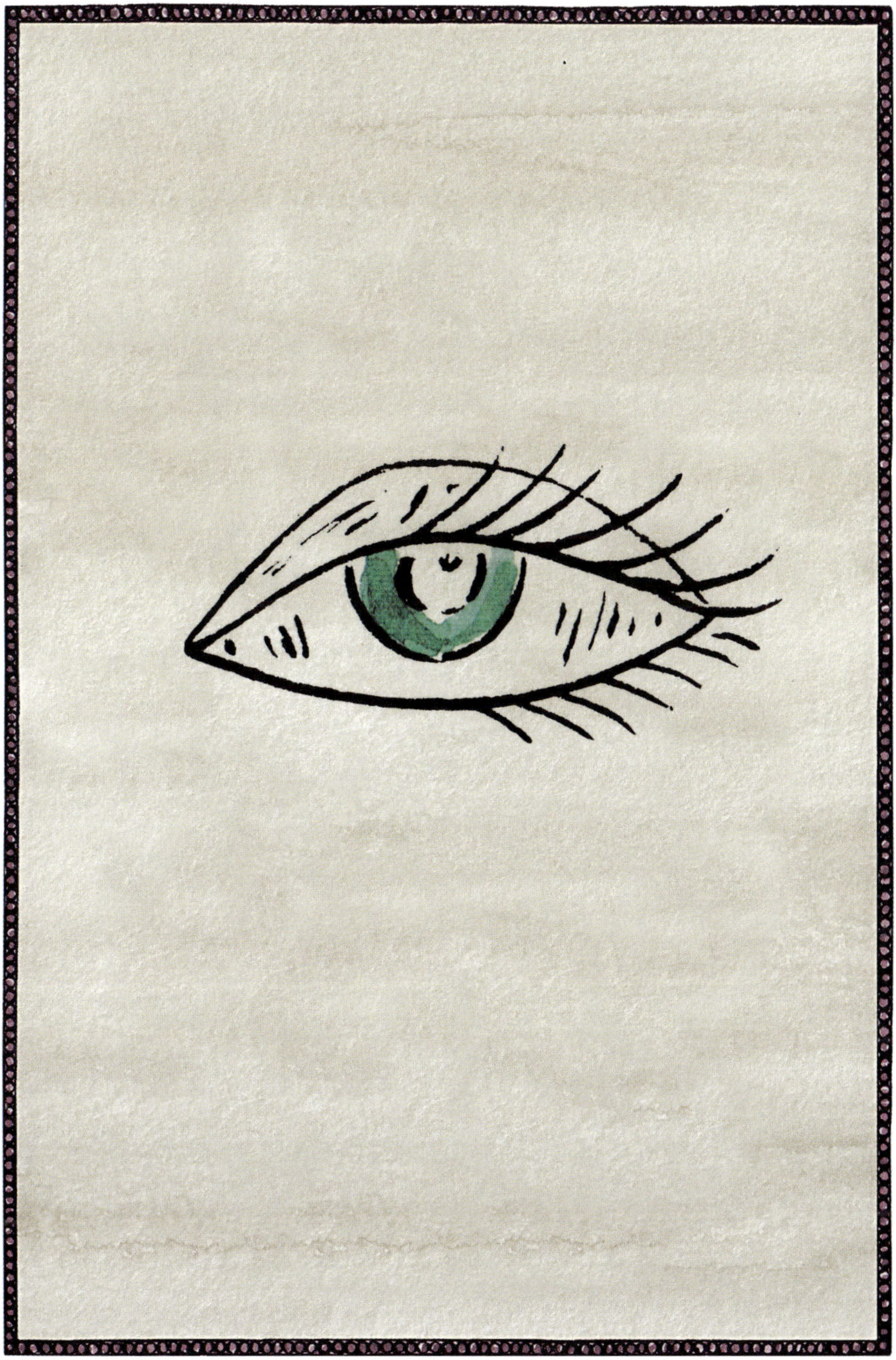

A SPELL TO BIND THAT BULLY

Not content with spreading rumours now your star power is on the ascendant, that particular someone has been dialling up the passive-aggression and bad-mouthing you whenever you enter the room.

So, what can you do about it?

This hex will help you take back control, end the trash talk and freeze out their influence on your life. The best time to perform it is during the waning moon, but if someone is upsetting you, forget the moon, reach for a lemon and put a stop to their nonsense right away!

MATERIALS:
A black candle
A slip of paper and a pen
A lemon
A knife
8 black peppercorns
Vinegar
A piece of tinfoil
Black string or cord

Light the black candle and start by writing down the name of the person you wish to bind on the paper. You could make the spell more potent by using a scrap of paper that they've touched. Roll up the slip until it is small enough to fit inside the lemon.

Cut the lemon in half and poke the paper into the middle of one piece. Press the peppercorns around it in a circle. Sprinkle a little vinegar over the cut halves of the lemon before pressing them together again. Black pepper is excellent for protection, while the vinegar will sour the bully's toxic words.

Wrap the lemon in foil, shiny side inward to reflect negativity back to its source, and then bind the lemon with the string. Tie at least four knots while reciting:

I bind you [XXX]

With this charm,

I freeze your power

and end your harm

Finally, put the lemon in the freezer. The bully's bad behaviour will be stopped and their negativity frozen out of your life.

FREEZE THEM!

Wherever you work, there's always one ... That person who's too loud, opinionated, or sarcastic, or whose 'jokes' don't land with the rest of the group. If you've tried the usual routes (a quiet word, an official complaint or totally ignoring the situation) and got nowhere, witchcraft can help. This simple spell will freeze their tricky traits and make them less of a disruptive influence. What's nice about it is that you're not being too specific about how this happens. Send your intention out there for the greater good of the group, and the Universe will take care of the rest.

Carry this spell out during the waning moon for the best results. It harnesses the power of Nordic runes, and you will combine two of them to make a binding rune.

Isa – to freeze

Algiz – for protection and defence

MATERIALS:
A photo of your problem person (either a printout or on screen)
A thick black marker pen or your wand

To carry out the bind, take the photo of your subject and focus on the negative qualities that you wish to freeze out. If you're using a printout of their photo, draw the runes across the person, saying, 'I freeze your sarcasm,' for example, as you draw Isa, then continuing the line down to form Algiz, saying, 'May this rune defend us from it.'

If you are working with an on-screen image, use your wand (or a drawing tool) to draw the runes across the picture in the same way. Keep the photo hidden away while the person is still a member of the team and dispose of it when you no longer need its icy power.

POPPET MAGIC

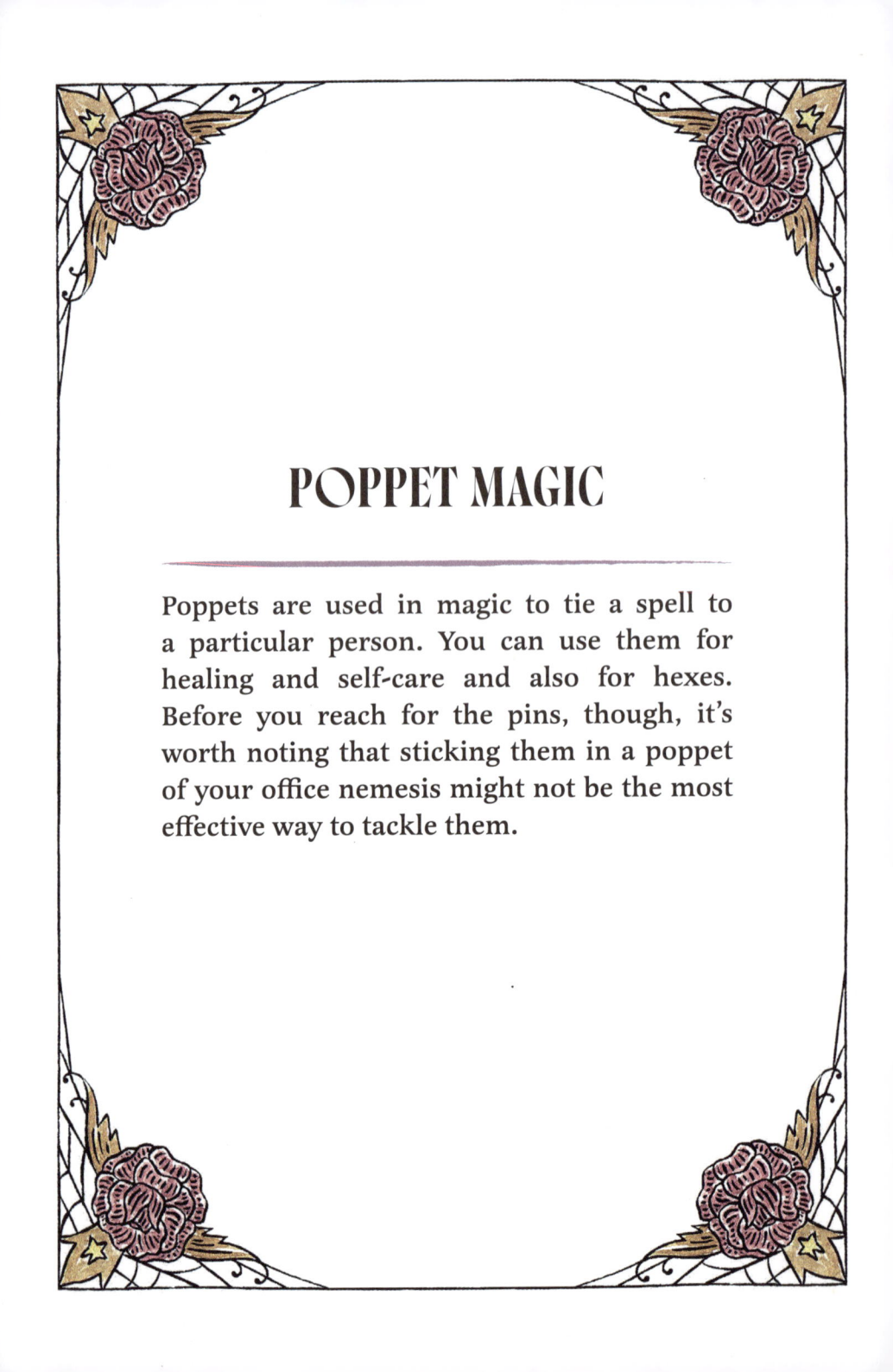

Poppets are used in magic to tie a spell to a particular person. You can use them for healing and self-care and also for hexes. Before you reach for the pins, though, it's worth noting that sticking them in a poppet of your office nemesis might not be the most effective way to tackle them.

Making a poppet

Poppets can be made from almost anything: wax, fabric, a Barbie doll, twigs ... Any three-dimensional representation of the person will work. You'll need to add a taglock to your doll. Traditionally this was a lock of hair or nail clippings from your subject, which linked the poppet to its person. You might not be able to sneak round the office snipping off people's hair, but you could use a piece of paper they've touched or add a label with their name on instead. 'Activating' your poppet is an optional stage and you could devise a naming ritual for it. Or if you prefer, simply crack on with the spell.

Hexing

For a simple hex, make a poppet of your enemy, light a black candle and ask that their bad deeds come back to haunt them, leaving the Universe to decide how that happens. You can be much more specific, though. If your enemy is greedy for attention, fill the stomach with a stone and ask that from now onwards they feel full, or if they truly deserve their comeuppance, you could use your imagination and add something baneful instead. You can also write your intention on paper and add that to the relevant area of the doll: 'May my supervisor feel empathy and kindness,' placed in the chest area, for example, could help them change their ways.

Binding spells

For an annoying co-worker who gossips all day, or speaks over you in meetings, make a poppet of them, and either ...

❖ Bind the mouth with tape or ribbon
❖ Paint over their mouth with correction fluid, or
❖ Place the poppet in a jar or under an upturned dish

... stating your intention to keep them quiet as you do so.

Disposing of your poppet

When your spell has worked, thank the poppet for its assistance and take it apart, cleansing and then disposing of the parts.

A BANISHING SPELL

That's it! You've had enough! You need to cut ties completely with someone who's causing you distress or who's behaved badly towards you. You don't want to leave your job, and why should you? They're going to have to go! Just to be clear, we're banishing them, not assassinating them, here!

MATERIALS:
A poppet (see page 144)
Some banishing oil (see below)
Paper and a pen
A trowel

FOR THE BANISHING OIL:
A jar
1 cup olive oil
A handful of cloves
A handful of pine needles

To make the banishing oil, cleanse the materials, then pour the olive oil into your jar. Add the cloves and pine needles, invoking their banishing powers, and let the oil steep on your altar for a week, or as long as you can, before performing the spell.

Make your poppet, adding details to identify your subject as clearly as possible. If the poppet is made of fabric, you could also stuff it with some autumn leaves to symbolize moving on, or cotton wool studded with more cloves. Write your intention on the slip of paper: 'I banish XXX,' and either stuff this inside your poppet or stick it on as a label.

Now anoint the poppet with the oil, keeping the rest for future spellwork, saying:

I ask that XXX leaves my life.
XXX be gone!

End your spell as you normally would by giving a few words of thanks, closing the circle, etc., and then take your poppet and bury it some distance from your home. The Universe will see to the rest!

QUICK-FIX HEXING TRICKS

Here are some speedy, subtle hexes to help get you through the week.

Nail 'em
If you know you'll be facing up to your office nemesis this week, nail art could be your way forward. Design a simple sigil to target their annoying traits – 'Let me speak' or, 'Stop being bitchy,' for example – and paint this on one of your nails. If you choose your middle finger, you'll get no judgement from me! You could use a significant base colour, too, perhaps red for power. When you encounter your enemy, subtly point the sigil their way and zap them with your intention.

Keep it compact

If a coworker is sending out negative vibes, a simple way to contain them is with some mirror magic. Buy a cheap two-mirror compact, cleanse it and set your altar up with a black candle. Use a small photo of the relevant person, draw a cartoon of them or simply write their name on a piece of paper. Fold this inside the compact, saying, 'Your words and bad vibes can do me no harm, I send them back to you.' Keep the compact until they change their ways.

Hard-boiled hex

Take a raw egg and use a permanent marker to draw on the initial of the person who has wronged you. Place the egg in a pan with a sprinkling of salt and cloves, to add cleansing energy into the mix. Boil the egg, thinking of any unpleasantness your colleague has caused as you do so. Remove the egg from the pan and pour the water down the toilet, sending your enemy's negativity away with all the other waste. Take the egg outside to a wild corner where rats or foxes might find it, or bury it loosely, saying:

The pain you caused is over

Your words no longer hurt,

The damage you created

Lies buried in the dirt

Start-up sigil spell

This simple hex uses the energy from your laptop booting up to boost your intentions. Design a suitable sigil for your hex – 'Banish XXX', for example – and draw this on a Post-it note. Attach it to your computer or laptop when you switch it on for the day and let the rush of energy send your intention out into the Universe.

AN ANTI-BITTERNESS ELIXIR

Some people raise the energy of a room just by being there, beaming out happiness and lifting everyone's spirits, and other people ... really don't. Bitter people give out negativity instead and, like a mouldy tangerine in the meeting-room fruit bowl, the gloom spreads around the team. This spell tackles the problem at its root by healing your colleague of any past hurts with a crystal elixir. And because we're healing them without their knowing, for the greater good of the team, it counts as a hex. Prepare the elixir at home and then use it to make their favourite hot drink at work.

MATERIALS:
A pink candle
A large rose quartz crystal or a handful
   of rose quartz tumblestones
A bottle of still spring water (enough to
   make a hot drink for your colleague)
Some sticky tape

This spell is based on the idea that water can take on the energy of nearby objects and intentions. Crystals are great for this as they have specific qualities that can be super-useful. As your cross colleague will be drinking this water, we'll be using the indirect method to infuse it.

Cast a circle and light the pink candle. Add any items to your altar that represent love and healing to you: perhaps a jade crystal, the Six of Swords or Star tarot card or some lavender flowers.

Hold the rose quartz crystal as you conjure a feeling of love, recalling a much-loved human or animal companion. Imagine the feeling flowing through you, then the crystal, then beaming out to connect with your loved-ones, family and friends. Now picture your workmate and beam this loving, healing energy towards them, too. Recite:

XXX I send you love

To heal all your past pain,

May your heart be filled with peace,

Find happiness again

Either tape the crystal to the water bottle or place it next to the bottle on your altar. Extinguish the candle, then leave the elixir to charge up overnight and use it the next day to make your colleague a drink at work. Beam love and kindness into the drink as you hand it over to them to set their healing in motion.

A 'TRUTH SHINES THROUGH' SPELL

Here's a spell to call out liars and gaslighters, and to ensure that the truth is heard.

MATERIALS:
A black candle
A toothpick or pin
A small cauldron or heatproof bowl
A small piece of red paper, cut into the shape of a tongue
A pen
A stapler
Some sage
A blue candle
A piece of lapis

Use the toothpick to inscribe the initial of the person who has been spreading lies at the top of the black candle. Warm the candle's base and, when the wax has melted a little, stand it firmly in the cauldron. Now, take the 'tongue' and write the name of the gaslighter along with 'liar' on it. Fold this three times away from you and put a staple through it.

Pour water into the cauldron to about two-thirds of the way up the candle and sprinkle in some sage (for cleansing and truth). When you're ready to begin, light the black candle and say, 'XXX, I call out your lies, may they die with this flame.' Next, carefully light the paper from the candle flame, saying, 'XXX, I bind your tongue, may you no longer speak ill.' Set fire to the paper and drop this into the water.

As you watch the candle burn down to be extinguished by the water, you may like to acknowledge or think about the lies that you are putting to rest.

When the candle has gone out, move the cauldron to one side and cleanse your altar. Next set up the blue candle, which represents your throat chakra and speaking the truth, and place the lapis at its base (lapis is also associated with honesty). Light the candle and either speak your truth aloud or journal about what actually happened to set the record straight. Finish by saying, 'May my truth be heard,' and thank the Universe for listening.

WITCHY WARNINGS

Here are a few reminders to keep you safe when you're getting Boss Witchy:

- Never leave burning candles unattended; always extinguish them safely at the end of a spell.

- If you're burning paper, bay leaves, or anything really, be sure to use a heatproof bowl and have some water to hand.

- Remember to dilute any essential oils with a carrier oil before adding them to your bath or your skin as they can cause nasty burns if used neat.

- If you're making an elixir, don't put crystals directly in water that you're going to drink as some can contain unpleasant chemicals that can be dangerous to ingest.

- Always cast a spell from a place of calm and positivity and always think before you hex!

BOSS WITCH BLESSINGS

I hope these spells empower you to take the next step ... make a change ... defend yourself ... bake some cookies ... find some comfort ... move onwards ... travel safely ... get your voice heard ... have fun ... and receive all the brilliant rewards you deserve.

The Boss Witch

INDEX

A
Altar (for abundance) 98-9
Altar (on the go) 116-7
Anti-bitterness elixir 150-1
Anti-stress ritual 112-3

B
Bad vibes (bottle them) 134-5
Balm (hocus-pocus, calm and focus) 52-3
Banishing spell 146-7
Besom (make a broom) 74-5
Binding spell (bully) 140-1
Brew (for balance) 68-9
Bright blessings (biscuits) 92-3

C
Candle (magic) 14
Candle spell (for harmony) 82-3
Charm, perspective 10
Coins 18
Colour magic 14
Confidence 38
Crystal magic 14, 46-7

D
Days of the week 30-1
Destressing ritual 60-1

E
Elements 86-7, 130
Energy tricks 72-3
Essential oils (room spray) 84-5
Evil eye (amulet) 126-7

F
Freeze-out spell 142-3

G
Glamour magic 62-3
Grounding stone 110-1
Guidance 18

H
Herbs 70-1
Hexing 120-1, 148-9

I
Imposter syndrome (how to banish) 56-7
Inspiration 28
Intuition 19

J
Job spell 40

INDEX

M
Money-drawing oil 102-3
Moon magic 24, 25, 26
Moon ritual ('losing the labels') 132-3
Money tricks 104-5, 131

O
Office romance (cord-cutting spell) 128-9
Oracle cards 16

P
Parking spell 114
Pendulum 19
Pentacle 106-7, 130
Poppet magic 144-5
Positivity (choc-orange positivity balls) 76-7
Positivity (tricks) 88-9
Potion ('hear me!') 58-9
Power through your to-do list spell 78-9
Power words 20
Prosperity (a simmer pot) 100-1
Protection (quick-fix tricks) 124-5

R
Rebirth 131
Recharge 26
Rejection ritual 136-7

S
Salary spell 96-7
Sigils (for success) 42
Smoke scrying 13
Spell bags 64-5
Symbols 130-1

T
Talisman (pick me) 44
Tarot (work-relationship reading) 90-1
Tech spell (for 'talking the talk') 48-9
Time management 32-5
Travel (quick-fix travel tricks) 54-5
Triple moon 130
Truth spell 152-3

W
Witchy warnings 154
Working from home spell 118-9

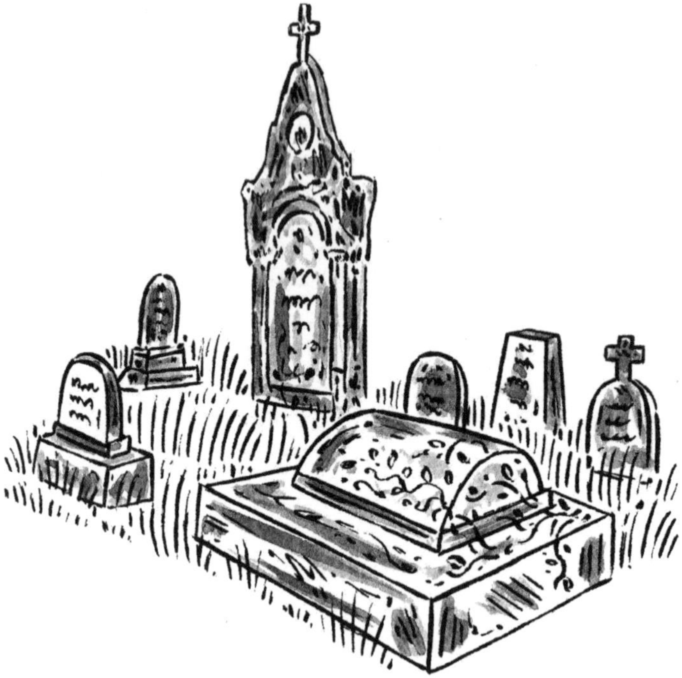